Israel Regardie
&
The Philosopher's Stone

Some Other Titles from Falcon Press

Joseph Lisiewski, Ph.D.
- *Ceremonial Magic & the Power of Evocation*
- *Kabbalistic Cycles & the Mastery of Life*
- *Kabbalistic Handbook for the Practicing Magician*
- *Howlings from the Pit*
- *Nightshadow (horror fiction)*
- *Geometries of the Mind (horror fiction)*

Christopher S. Hyatt, Ph.D.
- *Undoing Yourself with Energized Meditation and Other Devices*
- *To Lie Is Human: Not Getting Caught Is Divine*
- *Secrets of Western Tantra: The Sexuality of the Middle Path*

Christopher S. Hyatt, Ph.D. with contributions by Wm. S. Burroughs, Timothy Leary, Robert Anton Wilson et al.
- *Rebels & Devils: The Psychology of Liberation*

S. Jason Black and Christopher S. Hyatt, Ph.D.
- *Pacts with the Devil: A Chronicle of Sex, Blasphemy & Liberation*
- *Urban Voodoo: A Beginner's Guide to Afro-Caribbean Magic*

Antero Alli
- *Angel Tech: A Modern Shaman's Guide to Reality Selection*
- *State of Emergence*
- *Experiential Astrology*

Peter J. Carroll
- *The Chaos Magick Audios*
- *PsyberMagick*

Phil Hine
- *Condensed Chaos: An Introduction to Chaos Magic*
- *Prime Chaos: Adventures in Chaos Magic*
- *The Pseudonomicon*

Israel Regardie
- *The Complete Golden Dawn System of Magic*
- *The Golden Dawn Audios*

For up-to-the-minute information on prices and availability, please visit our website at http://originalfalcon.com

Israel Regardie
&
The Philosopher's Stone

By
Joseph C. Lisiewski, Ph.D.

Introduced by Mark Stavish

THE *Original* FALCON PRESS
TEMPE, ARIZONA, U.S.A.

Copyright © 2008 C.E. by Joseph C. Lisiewski, Ph.D.

All rights reserved. No part of this book, in part or in whole, may be reproduced, transmitted, or utilized, in any form or by any means, electronic or mechanical, including photocopying, recording, or by any information storage and retrieval system, without permission in writing from the publisher, except for brief quotations in critical articles, books and reviews.

International Standard Book Number: 978-1-935150-89-3
ISBN 978-1-61869-890-2 (mobi)
ISBN 978-1-61869-891-9 (epub)
Library of Congress Catalog Card Number: 2007938082

First Edition 2008
First ebook Edition 2012
Second Printing 2023

Cover design and illustration by Linda Joyce Franks

The paper used in this publication meets the minimum requirements of the American National Standard for Permanence of Paper for Printed Library Materials Z39.48-1984

Address all inquiries to:
The Original Falcon Press
1753 East Broadway Road #101-277
Tempe, AZ 85282 U.S.A.
(or)
PO Box 3540
Silver Springs, NV 89429 U.S.A.
website: http://www.originalfalcon.com
email: **info@originalfalcon.com**

Dedication

With fond recollection and deep gratitude, I dedicate this book to the memories of Dr. Francis Israel Regardie and Frater Albertus, my Teachers and friends to whom I owe so very much. Regardie's joy of life and dedication to the Great Work through both the Golden Dawn and the Old System of Magic inspired me, while the private tutoring he gave me over the last fourteen years of his life opened the vistas of my mind and spirit to Magic and Kabbalah in a way I could never have achieved alone.

Frater's balance of mercy and severity, his demanding attitude toward the Alchemy he taught, and the fact that he put me to task in this Art and Science on more than one occasion, kept me focused on the work at hand, the Work to be accomplished within, and that which had to be fulfilled in the laboratory without.

Between the two of them, they provided me with the magical, kabbalistic, and alchemical knowledge and outlook I have today. To you, my dearest of friends, I dedicate this effort.

Table of Contents

Introduction
    by Mark Stavish 9
To the Reader
    Some Important and Critical Remarks 15
Preface 23
Chapter One
    Israel Regardie and His Alchemical Beginnings 27
Chapter Two
    Israel Regardie & Frater Albertus: A Not So Chance
    Meeting 41
Chapter Three
    The Alchemic Art Brought Down to Earth 69
Chapter Four
    Israel Regardie & the Herbal Kingdom of Nature 91
Chapter Five
    Israel Regardie & the Animal Kingdom of Nature & the
    Formation of the Trinity 117
Chapter Six
    Israel Regardie & the Mineral Kingdom of Nature 133
Chapter Seven
    On the Generation of Animals 155
Chapter Eight
    On the Experimental Aspects of the Homunculus 179
Chapter Nine
    Clouds on the Alchemical Horizon 203
Epilogue 215

Introduction

by Mark Stavish

When Dr. Lisiewski first asked me to write the introduction to *Israel Regardie and the Philosopher's Stone* my first thoughts were about how strange the world of magic and alchemy is. Strange not only in the people we meet and the relationships that are formed, but strange in the way things work out. It is said that a straight line rarely forms in nature, and it is rare that magical acts, and relationships for that matter, follow a straight course. Curves, dips, peaks, and side-shots right out of left field are more often the case than not. My first meeting with Lisiewski was over 10 years ago and is a perfect example of this kind of phenomena. I received an email from Lisiewski and was impressed with his stated relationship with Regardie and Albertus. I turned off my computer with the intention of replying the next day only to have my hard drive crash. By the time everything was up and running again the email was no longer saved by my internet provider and I moved on to other things to make up for lost time. Now fast forward to 2005. I was doing some research when I came across Lisiewski's book, *Ceremonial Magic & the Power of Evocation* (The Original Falcon Press). Given his biography and being a resident of central Pennsylvania I emailed Lisiewski through his publisher on the off-chance that he was the same fellow who emailed me years earlier. For some reason however, it took another year before the original email a decade earlier from Lisiewski to me ever came up in conversation. Conversations between us that were held once or twice weekly, often for several hours, over the same period of time.

Lisiewski's experience with Regardie was not much different. On one occasion he mentioned that Regardie told him that he rarely answered the mail he received, and those that he chose to reply to were selected by holding the envelope to his forehead. If there was some kind of positive response, the letter was acknowledged, if not, it was thrown out unopened. Considering the content of Lisiewski's letter—a complete description of his first evocation to physical manifestation—it would not be surprising if Regardie got a migraine headache lasting several days from using this method!

Again, magic, like the energies of life of which it is a part, does not work in a straight line in most instances.

Over the last two and a half years a firm friendship between myself and Lisiewski has developed. It is rare to find operative magicians and alchemists in the former coal regions of Pennsylvania, but we do have them, and unlike their hip, urban, West Coast cousins, they are serious, quiet, and potent in their work: many even becoming local legends in their own lifetimes. Dr. Frederick Santee of Wapwallopen, Pennsylvania is one that comes to mind. A child genius, he was a cross between Doogie Houser and Harry Potter. He could read English and German when he was three years of age, translated Caesar's *Gaulic Wars* at the age of six or seven, and graduated from Harvard *magna cum laude* when he was seventeen. He would later go on to earn two Ph.D.'s and an M.D. An internet search will reveal a thing or two about him, including his esoteric activities. He traveled Europe in the 1920s and 1930s and in the late 1960s and early 1970s, Sybil Leak—astrologer, witch, and assistant to super sleuth Ian Fleming during World War Two—was a regular visitor to his out-of-the-way residence.

I bring up Santee because he ran in many of the same circles as Regardie, Crowley, and Frater Albertus. He was a contemporary of theirs, and it is said that he met the first two men when in London.

Yet, like Albertus at the end of his days—when the lodge he had built and put so much energy into was going to meet its ultimate test of survival without its founder—he uttered similar thoughts that we find Regardie stating here. If he had to do it all over again, Santee said he would forget magic and focus only on making money. As a physician Santee had a comfortable life, but it is also clear, that for all his occult skill and talent, in the end, he believed that the results did not justify the time and energy he put into it.

Magic as we shall see, truly is ephemeral. It is an illusion. It can be an illusion that serves us, instructs us, or destroys us. But be clear, it is an illusion. A veritable siren call causing many a life to crash on the rocks of despair and disappointment, and even madness. The lives of many gifted and intelligent men and women have been wasted in an obsession with the supernatural.

From the nonsense that is peddled about in the anemic and incestuous 'occult community' these days, and particularly those claiming the Golden Dawn mantel, or heir to Regardie's throne (or even Albertus' for that matter), this book will be anathema. Both men felt strongly that most of their students—be it in magic or alchemy—were dabblers, and both were tired of the 'artistic' nature modern occultism was being reduced to. Regardie and Albertus apparently believed, although in their own ways, that a more scientific rigor was needed, and that scientific thinking and methods should be emphasized over the highly subjective realm of personal interpretations. If an occult law was at work, then it was a law, *and* it had to be treated and understood as such. For both men, and like others before and after them, those who sought to be their students were often the source of their biggest sorrow in life.

I have little doubt that charges will be made and accusations stated against the author (and I am sure myself as well for having written this Introduction) that he is wrong. For the record, Dr. Lisiewski has many qualities, some of which we would consider nice, and many some would consider not so 'nice.' Among his nicer qualities is that he is a compulsive note taker, letter writer, and packrat, allowing him to document what he says. His wife who has suffered dearly through his occult explorations (as have too many wives of other occultists), was tasked with finding and organizing much of the material that was used to fact check this book. These notes came not from internet sources or published writings, but from the author's own archives, which include the paper Regardie wrote for his 5=6 Adeptus Minor grade, a copy of *The Goetia* given to him by Crowley and whose illustrations were colored in by Regardie, and even Crowley's copy of *The Book of the Law*. The list goes on.

Like Paracelsus, Lisiewski is also a bombastic egotist who admits this point freely to any who stay around long enough to know him, and that he is difficult to deal with, in large part because he is rarely wrong and he takes great delight in this fact. Whether gifted with, or through personal effort, he has an amazing memory and can recall conversations nearly word for word that passed decades ago. Those fortunate, or foolish enough, to know him find his wealth of personal and direct experience in a variety of difficult and arcane occult matters staggering.

Among the areas of occult research carried out by the author are some of the darkest and most neglected operations regarding the very essence of life itself. As the reader will see, it was under the direction of Albertus that Lisiewski worked on creating the legendary homunculus. For those brave enough to undertake the work of autocreation, full instructions and details are provided within these very pages. There is also sufficient introductory material on spagyrics to make this book a concise introductory to alchemy as well. Combined with the reference works he cites and his own instruction given herein, the intelligent and determined reader can most certainly succeed in his or her alchemical pursuits, whatever they may be. It may also surprise many readers to find out that Regardie was familiar with this 'diabolical' operation for decades and saw it as a possible link to the famed qabalistic creation of the golem, but like laboratory alchemy itself, dismissed it until he met Frater Albertus. A meeting made possible by the magical community's favorite organizational whipping post—the Rosicrucian Order, AMORC. While I have discussed the role of AMORC in the 20th century alchemical revival elsewhere, it is here, in this book, that many of the details regarding Albertus, Regardie, and their relationship are filled in. Like magic itself, this too was not a straight line, but one of delays, denials, and fruition after the initial impulse was forgotten.

As we stand at the entrance of the 21st century, it is no surprise that there are those who attended classes at the *Paracelsus Research Society* (or *Paracelsus College* as it was renamed) and are now just writing books on alchemy. However, no one has yet to write about what went on at PRS or about Albertus as a mystic, teacher, or a human being, and of Regardie as a devoted aspirant and co-worker with Albertus in the secret and yet practical world of laboratory alchemy. When we consider that Lisiewski was among the few people who knew both Regardie and Albertus on a personal level for 14 and 11 years respectively, and was privy to the personal communications between both men, in short, no book was written because no one other than Lisiewski could write it.

Future generations will be glad this book was written even if those who prefer to deny the humanness of these two great luminaries would rather it never saw the light of day. Yet for all of their warts and foibles, we can each see a bit of ourselves in Regardie, Albertus, and even Lisiewski too, as they travel the road in search of the Philosopher's Stone.

Mark Stavish, Director of Studies
Institute for Hermetic Studies
Wyoming, Pennsylvania
7 August 2007

To the Reader

Some Important & Critical Remarks

This is not a standard book as far as format is concerned. The text switches from a scientific reporting and documentary style, to expressions employing narrative with historical commentary overtones. This was deemed necessary to convey not only the complexity of the subject of alchemy, but the complex nature of Israel Regardie and his involvement with alchemy, Frater Albertus, the Paracelsus Research Society, and with myself, over a period of several decades. I trust it will be a pleasant read for you. But mark me well, it may not be an easy one. Not if you are trying to understand something of the man, Israel Regardie, his history in this matter of alchemy (and to a more limited extent, his history in magic), those who influenced him in his alchemical outlook, and those with whom he worked in this very fascinating field of occultism.

When Christopher S. Hyatt and I initially discussed the possibility of my writing this book in 2004, I had pretty much set my mind on doing so by engaging in a process we use in advanced mathematics: that of rigorous analysis. But instead, I thought I would apply this analysis to alchemy by directing it to the contents of Regardie's book, *The Philosopher's Stone*. That is, I intended to take his symbolic and mystical interpretation of the three alchemical texts discussed there, *The Triumphal Chariot of Antimony, The Six Keys of Eudoxus,* and *The Golden Tractate of Hermes*, and elaborate upon them in terms of the theory and praxis (practice) of alchemy as taught to me by Frater Albertus over a seven year period at the famous Paracelsus Research Society (abbreviated as PRS then and now) in Salt Lake City, Utah. That is why the original copy for this book's advertisement was initially worded the way it was on Falcon's website. Both they and I thought it would be just as Hyatt and I discussed.

But after taking pencil to paper, I soon realized that such an effort would be too vast to fit into the confines of a single volume. Much, too much alchemical theory would have to be presented to allow for an explanation of the praxis side of these three alchemical texts, not to mention a rather exhaustive rendition and careful explanation of the concepts that lie behind the terms used in the Science and Art that is alchemy. At the very least, three or more books would be required to even attempt such a task. And clearly, that was neither Hyatt's nor my intention.

So, what to do? This was the reason for the delay in writing this book. Just as a circle has no beginning or end, the problem continued to loop back upon itself, leaving me with nowhere to go in this writing effort. But really, this was not true. I was deceiving myself, and in the deepest recesses of my own mind I knew it. It is just the way of things. For there are those matters that haunt all of us for one reason or another, and which we dare not approach consciously lest we have to face secret issues we would rather keep carefully tucked away, hidden safely and conveniently in our own little closets of memory. This was one such issue for me. For while it might seem like a small matter to the reader, what I am about to reveal in this book is so psychically charged for me as to be painful in certain areas of its writing, and again, for my own private reasons.

To the best of my knowledge, neither Regardie nor Frater Albertus ever discussed the formal relationship which I am going to expose here. This is a relationship that the three of us established among ourselves, and directed exclusively into alchemical pursuits. Yet no small amount of detail of the nature, methods of operations, and results of those alchemical laboratory pursuits will be given.

Thus, it will remain for the reader who has eyes to see, combined with a certain understanding of the theory and praxis of alchemy, to take from this book *all* that he or she will. Thus, everything reported in this book is taken directly from my extensive class notes during my years at the PRS, from my private letters and conversations with Frater Albertus over the eleven-year period of our involvement together, and from my massive written communications and personal discussions with Israel Regardie. In no case have I filled in the blank with something convenient. This book stands as a representation for just what it is offered as: a historical account of Israel Regardie, his interest and work in alchemy, and his role and interaction with Frater Albertus and myself in this occult pursuit.

Let me make a few things clear. During the time I attended the Seven Year Cycle of Classes at the PRS—1975 through 1980 (I took two classes back-to-back in 1979)—Regardie himself was a student there as well. He, like the rest of us, worked under the direct supervision of Frater Albertus. He and I were not in the same set of classes, but communicated and exchanged our laboratory reports and lecture notes with each other, after each class, each year, and with Frater's permission. This was only after the *three* of us discussed those notes and reports *thoroughly.*

It came to be that the mystical and occult influence that dominated each of the classes—that of Frater's personality, his Teachings, the Interior working to which Regardie and I set ourselves, and the experimental laboratory work itself—radically and forever became the causal agents which gradually forced Regardie to change his views not only on the true meaning and purpose of alchemy, but on the very credibility of the Golden Dawn teachings in this matter. For as it turned out, this complex set of causes brought Frater Albertus, Israel Regardie and I together such that each, at his own residence during the twelve months between successive classes, carried out certain experiments that were both part and parcel of the previous year's class.

But there was more to it than that. In 1978, Frater Albertus, Israel Regardie and I formed a 'Trinity' of our own: one that was dedicated to exploring some of the darkest corners of alchemy. Yes, we continued to carry out 'routine' experiments on antimony and lead, the Green Lion, preparation of the Philosophical Mercury, and other exhaustive experiments from the contents of Valentine's, *The Triumphal Chariot of Antimony* and *Last Will and Testament*, and on some of the writings of Glauber. But in the main, the occupation of our Trinity was to test the claims made by alchemy's darkest—not principles—but tenets. Thus, a distance learning program of a sort was established between the three of us. One that would lead to two publications of my own appearing in Frater's, *Essentia: Journal of Evolutionary Thought in Action*, which will be reprinted in this book in their entirety, along with the presentation of other work I carried out under Frater's guidance, with the work on the Homunculus being of special importance.

This is the purpose of this book: To lay down an unknown part of alchemical history by providing historical information; an elaboration of the discussions that passed between Frater Albertus, Israel Regardie and myself; experimental instructions on some of the more interesting aspects of the dark corners mentioned; and a critical overview of the men who composed the Trinity. At the same time, the reader will find an account of those personal matters that brought Regardie and Frater Albertus together, as Regardie personally explained to me during our fourteen-year magical and alchemical association. Admittedly, there is much in this brief section. But if the sincere student desires to gain all from it that I have intended, then a careful study of it is not only warranted, but essential in *understanding* and *comprehending* what is to follow.

In closing this part, I would like to make something else perfectly clear as well. This may raise the hackles of a few, and upset others all the more, if for no other reason than because of the concept that sensitive people don't bring up such things. I do. I am not sensitive, and I do so because the time has come to put all of the nonsense of warm and fuzzy away, and get on with the *work* at hand—which is the accomplishment of the **Great Work** itself.

A number of books have recently appeared on the subject of alchemy. Some books are written by individuals who attended classes of the PRS with me. I find it disturbing to the nth degree that these same individuals never did a lick of work in alchemy either while in residence at the PRS during the classes, or during their twelve months away from the Society between successive class periods. Nor did these people ever commit a single word Frater Albertus uttered during those intense two-week periods to paper. Don't forget, these individuals and I sat across from each other during the lectures, and stood side-by-side during the laboratory periods, which ran around the clock but from which they disappeared as soon as Frater turned his head.

Frater also had a mandatory "Show and Tell" session. This was a three-day period at the start of each year's class during which he would take the individual's seat in the lecture room and they would have to take his at the front of the room. There, for an agonizing, undetermined length of time, they had to show what they did over the past twelve months and explain the results to the class and to Frater. In not one instance did these current authors ever have so much as a piece of glass of antimony to show, nor a botched Herbal Stone experiment to discuss. Instead, they spent that God-awful time discussing the latest love of their life, or how Frater's practical laboratory alchemy was helping them rise on the planes. (I can still see the expression on Frater's face during these discussions.) Now, these same individuals are writing 'books' on the subject.

A close friend and colleague of mine in these matters suggested that these same writers may have indeed changed their attitude and behavior in the ensuing years, and actually did the laboratory work later on. That may be, but I cannot prove or know it as a fact. All I can prove to myself and know is that when someone has the resources at hand; when they have the Teacher of all Teachers in the same room and laboratory with them and they do not make use of those resources, I find it incredulous that those same types suddenly 'saw the light' and went into the back-breaking work that *is* alchemy after the Society and Teacher passed from existence! I mention these seemingly irrelevant points as a warning to those few who truly wish to tread the Path of Alchemy. Be careful of the contemporary texts from which you work. Know your author well, lest you learn the hard way that all that glitters is not gold!

There are many out there who claim to know what they are doing and who say they have done the work. All that remains for the sincere student to do is to put the writings of those individuals—and mine—to the one, single test. It is the single experiment I have insisted upon throughout all of my magical books and occult writing. Ask, *"WHERE ARE THE RESULTS?"* No other test than this has to be applied to anything in life, including this most important of all endeavors.

Remember this. Test not only this book and what is claimed therein, test the one who wrote it as well. You can do this. Test *both,* and without even entering a laboratory—at least, at first. Test the book and the writer by *listening to his written words, and carefully feeling what they incite within you.* You will soon find out if you are reading words of truth, or at least, of fact. For the *energy* within those words, and the knowledge they convey, *must* make an unmistakable and undeniable hard impression on you. They must snap you out of your self-delusion and self-illusion by making you realize who you are, and who you are not, at the present moment; what you are and what you are not in that specific moment of time. You must be thrilled, but only by the prospect of becoming more by doing the hard work you are reading about. If the words don't inspire you in this way; if your immediate response to them is one of hope and love and light that makes you soar to the heights of fantasy at all the marvels you can achieve with as little effort (or pretended effort) and study as possible, rest assured you have come across a convenient presentation and a not-so-clever contrivance meant to sell a book. The rest is up to you.

Preface

From its earliest beginnings in Egyptian times, Alchemy has captivated the imagination and dedication of many individuals throughout the ensuing ages. Its complexity and mystery attracted the serious attention of such scientific minds as Sir Isaac Newton, the Father of Classical Mechanics in physics and one of the two co-discovers of the Calculus; to such religious figures as the Benedictine monk, Basil Valentine; to the medically minded Theophrastus Bombastus Paracelsus who has been hailed by some as the Father of Modern Medicine. Indeed, the full spectrum of intellectual, educational, and motivational levels of enquirers can be found in that fold designated as Alchemy. Today, Alchemy is still popularly viewed as the means to physical immortality, a way to achieve untold wealth by turning such base metals as lead into gold, or as a source of secret processes locked in arcane images that pictorially define the field, and through an understanding of such the individual can unlock their spiritual nature and enter into the Kingdom of Heaven while still on this earth.

To some extent, the legitimate work that underscores such alchemical quests does indeed support such fantastic imaginings and human longings. But to a much greater extent, the practice of true Alchemy—both in the study of it, its theoretical underpinnings, and in the application of that theoretical base in the laboratory—has little to do with these idealized and much longed for results. In fact, what Alchemy does offer—at least in the immediacy of its pursuit—is a philosophy and a series of applied techniques, the application of which has provided people of all times the ability to improve the health of their bodies, minds and emotions while strengthening and expanding their intellectual facilities, developing their imaginative faculties, and as a means of gaining a deep, genuine spiritual insight into the glories of their own being and the mysteries of Nature. And all through hard, diligent study and practice, not through fad meditation techniques supposedly designed to 'open the gates of alchemical symbolism' to attain an awareness of the Godhead within them, with such an attainment eventually leading to that Experience wherein they *consciously* unite with their own hidden, divine nature. This union brings such an all-encompassing and sweeping change with it, and in such a universal sense, that the individual's vision of entering into the Kingdom of Heaven while still on this earth becomes an Interior and Exterior Reality for them.

This is what Alchemy is all about. It is about studying the ancient manuscripts *after* having been enlightened with the hidden meanings of this Art and Science. It is about the practice, when the student takes the newly gained knowledge and converts it into Wisdom by applying this knowledge through the careful use of physical techniques which are an embodiment of occult forces and meanings inherent in the very processes the student is working with. It is about the perfection of the knowledge through further practice in the laboratory, which feeds back upon the knowledge, converting it into still higher forms of Wisdom. It is about obtaining ever higher manifestations of substances in the laboratory, which reflect this Higher Wisdom, and which leads to the Gates of the Green and Red Lions, and eventually, to the *summum bonum* of our Work: the Stone of the Wise itself, that is, the Philosopher's Stone. And in the end, it is about making manifest all those impossible and absurd dreams and imaginings that were the gleam in the eye of the student when the long, hard, and arduous journey into the secrets of this strange Occult Science was begun so long ago.

These are the grains of gold that lie at the heart of all true alchemical pursuits. They are also markers along the way in a developmental and evolutionary exercise that was first entered upon for wealth, physical immortality, fame, or power, but which in the process of working resulted in a spiritually transformed individual. One who in the end, can and does achieve those absurdities and fancies that were the initial drive into this arcane art and science. Yet, as the limit of possibility and believability is achieved, the heart is so changed, that the Philosopher—no longer the student—simply takes and uses those absurdities and fantasies now turned into realities, but only as one chooses and requires. In addition, the accolades and rewards of men and their world are of no further use whatsoever, as they are now seen as the beads and baubles of a discarded negative ego.

This is what real Alchemy is about. This, and no more. I trust that you who read these words take these ideas and expressions to heart. For if you do, your Path in Alchemy will be made straighter, if not easier. And eventually you will reach the end of that long road and confirm through your own spiritual unfoldment and laboratory results what I have written here, and that you do so to your absolute joy and understanding.

Chapter One

Israel Regardie & His Alchemical Beginnings

To set the stage aright and establish the background against which Regardie was brought to alchemy, I think it is necessary to name those conditions which were incited in Regardie and which flowed from general alchemical literature and ideas on the subject. One might study a historical compendium of alchemy, and while such a study can provide insight into the ebb and flow of the subject and its personalities, it does so in a static way. That is, it does not allow us to see into the human promptings such 'antiquated' facts, ideas, and ideals created in people who were brought up under its influence. And here especially, we are concerned with the impressions those forces made upon Israel Regardie during the early and later formative years of his life, circa 1933 to 1968. I establish this timeline based upon discussions with Regardie on this matter throughout the years of our relationship (1971 to 1985), which is covered in detail in my book, *Ceremonial Magic and the Power of Evocation*.

What is to follow is an attempt to give the reader some insight into the sequence of internal events and outer considerations that propelled him into the study of laboratory alchemy, not the mystical mumbo jumbo he had originally believed this art and science to be. Let the reader imagine that what follows in this present chapter are the expressed thoughts of Regardie as he related them to me, coupled with my reaction to them. Written in a conversational style, the manner in which Regardie approached alchemy after so much trial and error will be revealed.

Some of my own gleanings and experiences are also included to flesh things out so that a more complete, clear picture of what passed between us concerning his interest in alchemy, and his eventual meeting with Frater Albertus, can be more easily understood. This is presented in the form of a narrative, which should make for easier reading, while providing no small amount of detail concerning the history Regardie and I shared in this matter of alchemy, Frater Albertus, and the PRS.

I think it is safe to say there is no branch of Occultism that is more misunderstood and abused than the Science and Art of Alchemy. From the confidence men of the Medieval era to those of today, from the well-meaning but ignorant attempts of the Middle Ages to those of the Renaissance period, to those of our own time, Alchemy has been framed against a backdrop of lofty dreams, impossible processes, and even more impossible results. All was meant to somehow gratify and satiate the deep inner longings for transmutation—be that of changing the chemical 'base' metals such as lead and tin into gold, achieving physical immortality through the production and proper use of the Philosopher's Stone, or in using the secret symbolism of Alchemy as a gateway by which the 'spiritual growth' of the soul could be encouraged, and all of this, by applying the arcane formulas and processes of Alchemy *first* to the inner world of the aspirant's being.

In recent times, schools of Alchemy arose. Whether they taught Alchemy through privately circulated papers, books, or even through correspondence course instruction, serious attempts were made to translate the hidden meanings of this work into the inherent dynamic it is believed to be: one that is capable of being demonstrated both in the inner world of the Alchemical Experimentalist, and in the outer world of his physical laboratory. And while many of these attempts were genuine, in all cases they relied upon the

Medieval manuscripts of such alchemical greats as Paracelsus, Glauber, Valentine, Homer, Kerckringius, Sendivogius, and others too numerous to mention. In all of these cases, the secret instructions—both in the practical laboratory sense as well as in the personal spiritual sense—relied upon ideas, concepts, symbols, procedures, processes, and manipulations, which were and still are, not clearly and completely understood by either mainstream Occultism or modern-day Chemistry. How could they be understood, since the original ideas and meaning behind much of this source material still remains shrouded in mystery? More often than not, what began as an earnest and high-minded attempt to perform an alchemical experiment in a physical laboratory, degraded into a metaphorical application of those instructions for use in some vaguely defined inner work or exercise meant to develop one's spiritual nature, whatever that may indeed be.

Thus, once again, even after all of this honest and sincere effort, Alchemy fell back into the shadows of Occult activity, study and research, save for its continued application to the spiritual nature of man; the subsequent results of which are all too easy to tie into a spiritual religiosity that simply used the rare alchemical texts as a substitute for some well-known religious text, such as the Bible or Koran.

But this situation changed with the advent of the Paracelsus Research Society founded by a German immigrant, Albert Richard Riedel, Ph.D. (1911–1984), or "Frater Albertus" as he preferred to be called by his students. While the exact date of the founding of the PRS is not clear, it is known that he emigrated to America in 1933, immediately after Adolf Hitler came to power (this timeline by his own admission during one of my classes with him). Additionally, we know that the first issue of the *Alchemical Laboratory Bulletins* covering the years 1960–1972 appeared as a hardbound volume in 1972, having been available prior to that time by subscription only. It was also in 1972 that these bulletins ceased. (A later production,

Parachemy, carried on the tradition established by the *Alchemical Laboratory Bulletins*. In my opinion however, they were not as meaningful or clear either in their content or instructions, as were the Bulletins.)

These bulletins were small black and white, as well as color, productions of alchemical processes, procedures, equipment and techniques, along with the underlying alchemical theory. They were the first true hallmark that made plain that which was formerly hidden in the realm of Alchemy. Always, these instructions stressed *practical laboratory Alchemy*. There was never any discussion of Alchemy pertaining to man's spiritual growth or development, neither in the bulletins, or in the in-residence classes he taught. (Although Astrology or 'Astro-Cyclic Pulsations,' as he termed his interpretation and application of this branch of Occultism, and Kabbalah, were taught as part of the curriculum. Additionally, a three-minute period of meditation was also held the first thing every morning before the start of class.) Even in the bulletins however, it was clear that the instructions necessary to bring Alchemy into the light of modern-day science—which was Frater Albertus' greatest desire—could not be fully and effectively taught through the written word alone, at least, not in the time period in which he found himself. (As the years went by however, he came to realize that modern technologies could impact the transmission of these ideas and processes, but saw that this task would be left for others to accomplish, proclaiming this during my final class in 1980.)

Indeed, upon reading many of these bulletins, it becomes clear that certain key concepts and instructions were still lacking, making the bulletins fully useable only by those he taught privately, in residence, at the time. In fact, when questioned about the value of the Bulletins as a source of alchemical instruction during my second-year class, Frater stated,

"Well, they're fine to give you the idea and to answer questions that come up when you're working in the laboratory. But you need much

more than that. You have to remember those bulletins were written by myself and the people I first taught, so they only reflect the general outline of **detailed** *work we did together in the laboratory. You need to be taught orally and shown the way in the laboratory by someone who has gone where you want to go. Until then, they will be of little use by themselves."*

It was circa 1965 that the fully operational Paracelsus Research Society we know today probably had its formal beginning. From 1960 (and even a few years earlier as will be discussed later) up to that time, while Frater Albertus was teaching private groups of early PRS students, he was also finding his own way in bringing to the world the secret knowledge that he somehow came to possess. This period, 1960–1965, also includes the accelerated development of his teaching techniques; his larger vision of the Society and how he would launch it into the world-at-large; the beginnings of building the substantial facility that would house larger groups of students in the years to come; and his extension of the range of students he would accept. Put into today's parlance, during that early five-year period, all was yet under construction. Still, even though all this was gleaned from personal conversations with Frater, it is difficult to grasp the exact timeline of the establishment of the Society, and to understand the evolution of Frater's mystical development which was indeed reflected in the laboratory processes.

For example, during my final seventh (Septa) year class which ended on Halloween night, 1980, he remarked,

"This is the end of the twenty-one-year cycle. All that I have had to fulfill has been fulfilled. Yours is the last class of that cycle, and so brings about the closure of the Great Cyclic time. There will be no more sets of seven-year classes. From now on, short sets consisting of three-year classes only will be held for those who come after you. Look around at each other carefully, for this is the final time all of you will be present together in one room. Some of you will fail in

this Work. A few **may** succeed. Still fewer **will** succeed. And for a number of you, your lives in the physical body will soon end. So, look carefully about you and remember this moment. Yours is the ending class of the Great Cycle, and I chose each of you specially to represent this ending for my own reasons. In time, a few of you will understand."

Aside from the powerful message when closing the convocation, it was clear that in his mind, the PRS had its beginnings in 1960, most probably the time he took his first and only student which he once stated as having done during the "early days of our beginning" as he called it. Yet again, he mentioned in passing during my Quarta Class that he took his "...first few students in 1959, and the laboratory work began." All we can say is that officially the PRS began in 1960, since its creator established that time as its formal beginning.

In regard to his own mystical evolution, he made no overt statements concerning spiritual growth—or spiritual unfoldment, my term for the Interior component of the alchemical process—as being necessary to succeed in practical laboratory alchemical work. This bothered Regardie since he was looking for a mystical—not magical—approach that would give him the "Keys to the Kingdom." (As we shall see in Chapter Two, Regardie surmised the reason for Frater's refusal to deal with mystical techniques. Still, it bothered him.) Yet his daily class theme during each of the seven yearly classes did allude to the necessity of this evolutionary inner process, but usually in very vague terms.

While there was never any discussion of his own Path of Unfoldment, he kindly tolerated all forms of spiritual and mystical schools of thought, clearly evident from the many side remarks made here and there during the classes. That is, he demonstrated an understanding and fatherly tolerance for all but one Path, the one to which he was vehemently opposed, and which he slighted and demeaned when given the slightest provocation. This would be the

Israel Regardie & the Philosopher's Stone

Path of Magic. I can relate a shining example of this that occurred during my fifth-year class. My roommate (who I shall refer to as Curt) and I performed the Lesser Banishing Ritual of the Pentagram (LBRP) privately in our dorm room at the PRS in the wee hours of the morning. We chose that late hour since all the other students in the dorm were asleep, and owing to an early class start each day at 8:30 AM, we knew that Frater would be asleep also. We proceeded with the ritual at 3:00 AM. At 8:30 AM, Frater did not stroll into the large, luxuriously decorated and furnished lecture room in the main building, ready to teach, as was his custom. To say that he stormed in, utterly furious and almost out of control, would be an understatement. He raved and screamed,

*"There are two here who know better than to do Magic on these premises! A Banishing Ritual of the Pentagram! That foolishness has never been permitted here and never will be! How dare you two do such a thing in this **special** place! You know who you are, and your fellow classmates know who you are from your reputations, so I will not have to point you out. But hear this and remember you were told! If this ever happens again, I will insist you pack your things and get out of this Society, never to return! Have I made myself absolutely clear?!"*

To this day, I can still feel the shame and humiliation I experienced during that dressing down. Curt and I had no idea how he knew what we did, or even how he knew the exact ritual we performed, as we did it in a sealed room when everyone was asleep. But Frater's ways extended far beyond the physical, which we experienced on that day and on many others. Needless to say, neither Curt nor I ever dared to do any Magic again while at the PRS. When I returned home from that class, I told Regardie about it. At first he laughed heartily, in that emphysemic way he had. But afterward he became serious and chided me severely, telling me,

"You know how Albert feels about such things! Why did you that? Don't you have any respect for another's wishes when you're on his property, and being taught by him yet? If I don't do such things when I'm there, don't you either! I'd better never hear of you doing something like that again! Because to tell you the truth, I wanted to see if you would own up to what you did by telling me. At least you did that right. But I have to tell you Albert already told me what you and that other fool did there. He was more upset than you know, and you better never do such a thing again!"

So why would this Alchemist accept Regardie as a student, years earlier, knowing his worldwide reputation in the field of Magic? Regardie was very perplexed over this and never had an explanation. Further, why then would Frater, years later, accept me, a magical protégé of Regardie's, for those same alchemical classes? For it was Regardie who, in October of 1974, arranged with Frater Albertus that I not only begin the cycle of seven-year classes in February of 1975, but that I begin the *final* set of the Seven Year Cycle Classes? A very big event in this matter, as Frater expressed during the 1980 closing convocation. In this matter too, Regardie was even more confounded over Frater Albertus' decision to admit me to the classes, even though he interceded for me.

As the reader can see, Frater Albertus and Israel Regardie were very complex men, and any attempt to read and decipher them and their motivations in a linear way was, and still is, an exercise in utter futility. Things were rarely black or white with either of them. Instead, the shades of gray they projected at all times, were all that one ever had to interpret.

Regardie's interest in alchemy began about the year 1933 as he explained to me in 1976. Our conversation on this matter started in an innocent enough way. But as you will see, it escalated almost out of hand, owing to Regardie's continued recollections during that conversation, as if his recollections had summoned up no small amount of animosity for those he saw as holding him back for

Israel Regardie & the Philosopher's Stone 35

decades from furthering his deep interest in the art and science that is Alchemy. And so he began.

"Even from my youngest teenage days I always felt there was more to it [alchemy] than meets the eye. The Golden Dawn [GD] material is all right. But somehow, all this magical stuff and Jungian psychology must be the tip of the iceberg. Oh, sure, I liked the Z.2 document very much when I was young. I even thought I got a lot out of it back then. But when it came to doing the practical work, it contained too much spiritual overtones and undertones. I came to view it as totally irrelevant as far as real instructions in the [alchemical] processes go. As far as I was—and still am—concerned, it always fell short. Way short. Just flat. You know what I mean? There was something there in this alchemy business to be sure, but what?

"Let me tell you those Temple Chiefs and so-called adepts of the Hermes Temple of the Stella Matutina I belonged to didn't help matters either! They were nothing but ignorant louts! [Regardie was prone to using some rather colorful expletives at times, especially when he was extremely irritated, frustrated, or angry. And this was one of those times. I have lightened up his colorful descriptions of the Temple Chiefs and Adepts to make it more palatable to the reader.] None of them, not one of those idiots were capable of doing any magic, let alone alchemy! So, I had done with them and almost with alchemy too back then!

"But the idea of the Philosopher's Stone, Green Lion, Philosophical Mercury, all that had too much of a ring of truth to it. I just knew there had to be more to all of this, so I continued to search. All of this originally got me looking into the possibility of doing some practical laboratory alchemy, but to no avail.

"You have to know too, that the Old Man [his affectionate term for Crowley] had a terrible influence on me here as well. If it wasn't Magic—**his** Magic—he simply wasn't interested. And his opinion of Alchemy? I mean, true, laboratory alchemy as opposed to spiritual alchemy? He told me I was a damn fool for even considering such a thing! Said I'd be better off perfecting my ritual work than I would be chasing after the shadows and phantoms that were Alchemy, and which were still being cast by the charlatans and fools of the middle ages! He convinced me, on and off as it were, that the lack of practical instruction in Golden Dawn Alchemy and other [then] contemporary material proved that Alchemy was allegorical in nature, and only had relevance in terms of spiritual growth.

"At other times he almost convinced me that the real laboratory alchemy was a thing of the past, lost with the likes of Paracelsus and that crowd, as he referred to the old timers [alchemists] with a sneer. And that what was available in the literature of our time was nothing more than watered-down, twisted distortions of the true but lost alchemy. He insisted the secret practice of true alchemy had become an occupation of dupes and scoundrels who simply wanted to turn lead into gold, or to convince their supporters they should fund them to do this. He was utterly beside himself whenever the subject came up! Even when I tried to use a spiritual interpretation of Alchemy with him he only sneered and said that it was nothing but magical principles in disguise.

"This had a much, much greater negative impact on me than did the laughable contents of the Z.2 document, and the idiots who posed as the Chiefs and Adepts of the Order! Don't forget, I was only in my early twenties, and took all of this stuff to be of vital importance in my life, and that I put all of the greats—everyone, even the Order Chiefs at one point—on pedestals approaching Godhead! Then this! Maybe now you understand why half of me wanted to pursue Alchemy while the other half was quite reluctant to really give it a go! It wasn't an easy time, I can tell you!"

I was both surprised and shocked to say the least when he told me this, mainly owing to my own age at the time. Only now do I realize that while I was discussing this matter with him I was only twenty-seven years old at the time, and he was sixty-nine! I was talking to a living, breathing, walking piece of history! Our roles were reversed. He was the Old Man now as far as I was concerned, and I was where he had been at during the period of occult history he was relating to me! I was desperate to know more, so I asked him why—if he felt all of these conflicting emotions and confused views—he wrote the book, *The Philosopher's Stone* in 1936–1937, with its first edition appearing in 1938? At the time it made no sense. His answer surprised me as well. (At that age, nearly everything surprised me.) Regardie laughed heartily and deeply and answered,

"Well, you know how is it, Joe! You start on something, go off on what looks good, and take it as far as you can. Sometimes you feel that if you do the work [here, write the book on the Philosopher's Stone], it will open up something to you and you will be able to go further with it. But that didn't happen. That's why I put the whole damn thing away for another twenty years. There was just nowhere to go with it. It was around 1937 I think. I was still young, around where you are now. I had the Golden Dawn to release, had other writing I wanted to do, wanted to learn more of psychotherapy, and was looking to establish a practice in it, and that was enough. I had more on my plate than I knew what to do with then. I still do!

"But I have to tell you in all honesty, there is one thing I think would have made a great difference in all of this. That's chemistry. What I mean is I don't have the chemistry background I feel a person really needs, to do laboratory alchemy properly. Oh, how I wish I had it! If I had it to do all over again, I would have never gone into psychotherapy and all that psychology business at all! But you know, hindsight is always easy. Still, that's where you have it over all of us! In your physics! I'm telling you, if I had it to do all over again, I would have become a chemist or a physicist or a mathematician, or even an astronomer. [Regardie loved astronomy very much.] At least the Hard Sciences would have given me the right mind-set to pursue these things! Not only Alchemy either! I mean

Magic as well! There are just too many things in all of this occult business that serves as fuel for fools and wares for charlatans! A good, strong scientific mind—or at least a sound scientific attitude—would have turned me around in a lot of this and made my life a hell of a lot easier!"

Disregarding his comment about having a full plate in front of him, I naively asked him why he couldn't have taken some college chemistry courses to get some of the background he felt was needed. His answer was short and to the point.

"I'm too tired these days and have too much that still needs doing, and I don't mean in Magic or Alchemy, either. As I said, I should have gotten the scientific background when I was your age. Now, it's too late for me."

I tried to find out the specific nuts-and-bolts as to why he found the GD material on alchemy insufficient. But all he would say to that was,

"It all sounds good, but from what I heard from other Order members of the Hermes Temple, there was nothing substantial to it. There were two or three chaps there I liked. At least they were earnest, and tried to do the magical work properly. But they had no help or support at all from the Chiefs and Adepts. It was disgusting. Really, I got the feeling that those fellows actually tried to work with the instructions given in the Z.2 document, but they came up bare and scrapped the whole thing. This is why I got the opinion I did of it. And they received no help from the high muckety-mucks. But since it was all part of the GD system, well, it was conveniently relegated to the closet out of embarrassment. Nobody ever talked about it openly while I was with the Order. It was just the same magical nonsense as usual, day after day, meeting after meeting."

But I knew Regardie well enough even in 1976. Our (then) five-year intense relationship in Magic, and his intercession to get me into the Seven Year Cycle of Classes at PRS, told me he wasn't being fully candid about this matter of Alchemy and why he really wrote the book, *The Philosopher's Stone,* an erroneous, spiritual 'tribute' to the fundamental laboratory *mis*-interpretation of what the *core* of Alchemy is truly all about. In very polite words I asked him if the publication date of 1938, so very near to his 1937 final break with Crowley, had anything to do with publishing a book that would set the Old Man off ten ways from Sunday. There was a long, intense silence.

His reply came in a muffled, low tone of voice, as if he were telling me some secret thing. Something that in some way he was ashamed of, to some extent. He finally replied.

"I wrote about the Old Man and why we broke. But nothing I wrote or ever will write is going to contain all of it. None of my writings ever included the entire bedrock of why we broke. It's a lot like a marriage gone bad. No one ever really knows what went on except the husband and wife who split. Well, all I'll say is he hurt me so much in the final flare up, that the book I was writing at the time, The Philosopher's Stone—which I was going to ask him to please consider endorsing even with his feelings against Alchemy—was part of the reason the argument became so violent and why we parted company forever. It was a part only, because there were other issues between us. So, what you've surmised is right. Really, **the Philosopher's Stone might never have been published after that break. But I was hurt so bad by what the Old Man said over everything, that it was my way of hurting him back, and declaring my freedom from him! I was telling him I didn't need him anymore! And more than that, my intention to ultimately release the Golden Dawn documents was an act I designed in order to tell everyone I didn't need any of them or anyone anymore!***"

At that point I ended the discussion. I saw that those questions, and the fact that I had pursued the subject in order to understand him and his desire to engage in laboratory alchemy better, had opened deeply buried emotions that were none of my or anyone's business. I remember thanking him quietly and apologizing for asking what was clearly none of my concern. He replied once more on the matter, in a low, guttural tone.

"That's all right. Maybe now you can set the record straight someday if you ever write a book on the subject, or on your own life in these matters."

Regardie's putting "...the whole damn thing away for twenty years...," thus can be seen as an unfortunate mix of the empty result of his early efforts to learn Alchemy from the Golden Dawn and its Z.2 material; Crowley's attitude toward Alchemy; Regardie's own ineffective but noble efforts to unlock the secret of practical laboratory alchemy himself; and collectively, from the ignorant, closed-minded influences exerted upon him by those he revered so highly. This then takes us to around the year 1958, when something happened. That is when a purposeful, planned action of Regardie's would set the stage for change—for Regardie, Frater Albertus, and eventually—sixteen years later—for myself as well.

Chapter Two

Israel Regardie & Frater Albertus: A Not So Chance Meeting

Before we can see into and understand the initial meeting that occurred between Frater Albertus and Israel Regardie, there is some background material about Frater Albertus which must be entered into. This framework will better enable the reader not only to understand the seemingly mysterious and generally unknown early alchemical beginnings of Frater Albertus, but the role that Frater's growing reputation in the 1950s had upon the maturing Regardie. A reputation which culminated in the two of them finally meeting, as a result of Regardie's carefully laid plan. This, as Regardie related to me in 1979. It will also shed what I trust is some not too little light upon Frater's early struggles when he immigrated to America; struggles that played an extremely significant role in shaping him into the indomitable individual he truly was.

Other reflections presented here are taken from Frater's own lectures delivered to those of us who attended the Sexta and Septa Classes of 1979 and 1980 respectively, and from personal discussions I had with him concerning these matters. While it is true that Frater was generally closed-mouthed about his early years in this country, this image of him is only true in so far as his refusal to communicate these details to those people whom he did not know very well, or who he distrusted. I am also personally aware of him giving disinformation to a few enquirers on this matter as well.

When I asked him why he simply smiled and said, "Because it's none of their concern." Again, this was according to his own admissions in those classes, and in private conversations with him.

As to his early formative years in Germany and later travels to France in the late 1930s to further his knowledge of Alchemy, he was equally tight-lipped to those he was suspicious of. Yet, when Regardie and I compared notes over these matters, we found the information he divulged to us privately to be rather scanty as well, although without discrepancy. With the stage set, let us now first turn to the man and Alchemist, Frater Albertus. Then, we will proceed onto the dynamic relationship that he and Regardie would establish over the twenty-six-year period, 1958–1984.

General consensus has it that Frater was born in Dresden, Germany, in 1911. When asked about this during one of the classes I attended, he smiled wryly, and avoided the issue of the date of his birth. Instead, he went into a dialogue that I copied down as exactly as I could. Then I cornered him about some of the details later, when we were alone. It was as if he knew that what he said would come out later in some way, since he spoke slowly and even more meticulously than usual. Consequently, some elements of the dialogue to follow are based upon that private discussion he and I had over this matter. It would make for a very difficult and awkward presentation if I were to differentiate the two, owing to similar material appearing in both discussions. To make for easier reading and a more even flow, I have simply combined the two discussions. Nevertheless, what is reported below is an accurate, verbatim account of what transpired over this topic. And so he began.

"I came to America in the 1930s by way of France, where I went to learn more of Alchemy. I had some background in it from some students of the subject I met in Germany during my very early years. But always it was insufficient. Most were concerned with the 'spiritual' aspects of the subject. They really didn't have any laboratory experience, but wouldn't admit to it. In fact, many of them outright

feigned that they did have such experience. It took me awhile to realize this, because I was so young and so entranced by the subject. But when I finally made up my mind as to their pretentiousness, I had done with the lot of them and moved on.

"But there was much more to it than that. Hitler came to power in January, 1933. Even before that, things were bad in Germany. People would just disappear overnight, never to be heard of or from again. There was also a patriotic feeling in the air that to me was very dangerous. People I knew—good, hard-working, honest people —suddenly began to point 'others' out as different and undesirable. They only whispered such things at first. But in a short time they became vocal, and then physical, refusing them service, cursing them, and in some instances, assaulting them openly. Mind you, this was in 1931 and 1932 before Hitler rose to the top. Once he did though, things got very out of hand. The Germans and the Germany I recognized were no longer there. Violent beings now inhabited those formerly loving, caring, gentle bodies of the people I knew. The spirit of nationalism was everywhere.

"There were changes everywhere one looked, from the highest levels of government to the small, country one-room school house. Everywhere, people targeted these others for their physical stature and general appearance, and killings became commonplace. By 1935 even some of those I knew who were involved in alchemy had joined the Nazi Party, and spoke of secret societies being formed within the Master Race, and how alchemy could help bring about a transformation of the German People, no matter where 'our' people live. It was at this point that I made up my mind to leave my beloved country.

"I knew deep within myself that war clouds would soon be on the horizon, and no part of Europe would be safe, because the statement, 'no matter where our people live' would eventually mean war and conquering other countries. Those countries and people would then be controlled too, as was everyone and everything in*

Germany. And if the Reich spread beyond its own borders, everything would not simply be controlled but severely controlled in all the countries conquered by the war that was coming. I was so certain of this that I made my plans by contacting others in France whom I met through my German constituents, and so moved there. But only temporarily. Remember, as I said, I was certain that all of Europe and even beyond was in great danger. The imminent peril of National Socialism and its racial base could reach only one conclusion as far as I was concerned.

"You have to know National Socialism is rooted in the concept of race, not economic control as was the case with Mussolini and Fascism. This made it worse. Why, even Mussolini used Jews in his government to stabilize and expand the financial growth of Italy and to exercise absolute control over the country and its finances. But that had no play at all with the Nazis. Their ideology was based solely on Blood and Soil, as they said, which invoked some of the most powerful and dark feelings in its party members and in the nation as a whole.

"After having made my plans I left Germany in the Spring of 1936 and moved to a small town not too far from Paris. There I remained for a year, contacting as many as I could and learning all there was available to learn of laboratory alchemy. But in the end, I found it was no more than I had learned in Germany. The French also were sold on the idea of Alchemy as a spiritual effort, with the keys hidden in alchemical symbolism. There were other problems too, ones that didn't come to my attention quickly because people there are so good at talking around issues. And these other problems were akin to those that existed in Germany. Many of the French Alchemists were collaborating with their German counterparts, trying to fit their alchemical ideals into the Nazi fold. By now everyone knew war was coming, including the French. So, the alchemists there were trying their best to take care of themselves *and their Art. What they did was to turn their label of Alchemy into one that read Occultism, just as their German contemporaries did.*

"You see, the Nazis did not like specific ideas. They hated astrologers and mystics, and even Christians. But the country was too christianized and had been for a millennium, so they stopped trying to replace Christianity with their Nordic pagan beliefs. They did need the people as a whole behind them, so they backed off when their Nordic paganism was openly rejected by the populace.

"But as to astrologers and mystics, they persecuted them, and openly. However, if someone had occult leanings they left them alone as long as they did not interfere with the Nazi ideas and the racial purity ideals of the Reich. In fact, for a time Hitler had an astrologer, but things didn't fare well there and I believe he had him executed. Still, if you were an Occultist instead of an Alchemist, you were bound to fare better—as long as you didn't push it too much. Why, even the SS had an occult branch and their own inner philosophy based on a type of dark mysticism. They even had a castle devoted to it where high-ranking SS Occult Officials met frequently. And from what I came to understand years later from two members of noble rank whose sons joined the SS as Officers, they even practiced gruesome rites in the castle before and after their meetings. These were rituals which were supposed to employ the skulls and bones of dead SS soldiers who died valiantly in battle.

"Therefore, because of all this, occultists were pretty much left alone. I had a rift with several of those who professed to be alchemists over this Nazi matter, how they appeased the Reich, and their 'work' in what they called Alchemy. That was near the end of my stay there, but it did serve as fuel for me to be on my way. So, when I left, I left for good, and was quite happy to be done with the lot of them.

"One of you asked if I came from Dresden. I came to America via France as I said, but from a small town in Germany, one surrounded with the beautiful, white snowcapped Alps. That is why I *decided to settle here in Salt Lake City, Utah. Quite simply, it reminded me of my home town, the beauty there, and the happy years I spent there as a child. [Note to the Reader: Frater would often do this. He would address a question only after introducing some background he thought important in understanding his answer. He did not act this way during those short lecture sessions given in the laboratory proper. Neither did he use this approach to direct questions asked in the formal lectures given in the main lecture room. However, in private discussion, or to elaborate an important technical issue in the main lecture room lectures, he would go into this extended mode of answering. As a general rule however, while in the laboratory or in its small lecture room in the laboratory, his answers were short, direct, and to the point.]*

"Contrary to what you may have heard, when I first came to America in 1937 I did not settle in California. My intentions all along were to settle in Salt Lake City permanently, and for the reasons I mentioned. Upon [yes, Frater did speak like this: his diction was flawless] establishing myself in Salt Lake with some relatives who were already living there, Soror Emmy joined me in Salt Lake. [He married Emmy, a German National like himself, in 1932.] But establishing myself here [Salt Lake City] was more difficult than I had imagined. It took several years to take care of this and some other business before I could make my way to California. But first there was this other business to take care of and so I was detained in Salt Lake City for several years. Nevertheless, I did establish contact with the Rosicrucian Order AMORC in those lost years, always with my eye on taking what alchemy they had to offer. Their original program had come very highly recommended to me by some friends I made while in France, and from two other Germans I worked with prior to leaving Germany.

"Finally, I began to take their alchemical classes of instruction through their Rose-Croix University, which was on the grounds of the Rosicrucian Order itself in San Jose. Their classes were com-

Israel Regardie & the Philosopher's Stone 47

*pletely practical, but still, they were incomplete. After two separate parting of the ways, they [AMORC] and I went our own ways in this matter of alchemy. They became very elementary in their approach to the subject in my view, their program eventually degenerating into selling the most basic Herbal Alchemy home working 'kit' one could imagine, from the early 1960s through the early 1970s. [There was an earlier home kit offered by AMORC that was anything but basic. It was offered about the time Frater and AMORC began to work together, i.e., the early 1940s. But after Frater's **first** break with the Order—referenced above—circa 1946, this advanced kit was still offered in the early to mid-1950s. Both others and I saw the original advertisements for these home alchemical laboratory kits, and they were not very elementary at all. Sometime in the late 1950s these respectable kits disappeared, only to be replaced by those Frater was making reference to above.] After that, I don't know what became of their alchemical program, as I had removed myself from it and all associations with them. And I was quite happy I did."*

These facts are also concerned with the **first** break he had with AMORC. All of this falls directly into line with other documents I came across years later, and which I have to this day. In fact, these documents show that Frater did indeed attend the alchemy classes at the Rose-Croix University of AMORC circa 1942–1944, and further, that he was taught by none other than Orval Graves, Librarian, who was very well versed in practical laboratory work as given in the writings of Paracelsus, and who lectured from the writings of Paracelsus directly, most notably from the massive tome produced by none other than A.E. Waite, entitled, *Hermetic and Alchemical Writings of Paracelsus the Great*. (This edition is still available from Kessinger Publishing. I have used it in my own practical alchemical work extensively, and can attest that there is nothing like it for those who have prior training in Laboratory Alchemy. Unlike so many other books purporting to give "…clear and detailed information in those processes by which Nature is exalted and glorified...," Waite's translation of Paracelsus' work truly does give the practical laboratory alchemist what it claims.)

I should also mention that additionally, I have come into the possession of yet other notes used at the time, circa 1942–1944. They are **identical** both in content and format to what later appeared in Frater's book, *The Alchemist's Handbook*. In the Handbook, Frater refers to receiving permission from Grand Master Thor Kiimaletho (a Finn) to quote from "Some Rosicrucian Concepts" (p22), thereby placing Albertus firmly in contact with AMORC prior to 1942, as Frater indicated to me and as I have noted above.

Sometime after 1944 then, there was a disagreement between him and AMORC proper. It did not reach a climax immediately, but rather, developed over the course of a two-year period. That is, Frater came to some major disagreement with the general leadership of AMORC, and not with Orval Graves, the Librarian who taught the practical laboratory classes, nor with the Rose-Croix University. Nevertheless, sides were taken by those involved at AMORC, with the ensuing, out of control disagreement upsetting Frater Albertus so much, he broke with the Order and returned to his wife and private life in Salt Lake City, sometime in 1946. But his life there was not quiet for long.

As he related in my Quinta Class of 1979—the first of the two classes I took back-to-back that year, along with the Sexta Class which followed—while at the Rose-Croix University, circa 1942–1944, he heard of an individual living in "...the wilds of Montana..." as he phrased it, who "...was deeply skilled in the practical aspects of Alchemy. It was so important to me, that I decided to spend quite a while with this man in Montana, learning all he had to teach. Finally, I returned to Salt Lake City, my family, and my business interests."

Other than this admission about studying under this mysterious Alchemist in Montana, very little else is known of Frater Albertus' personal activities between 1946 to 1955. That is, nothing except becoming involved in some businesses back in Salt Lake City that allowed him to continue his private alchemical studies and work, and provide for his wife and ever-growing family. (He and Soror are said to eventually have had five children, at least, this was the number reported by others during the classes I attended at the PRS. If this subject was broached with Frater however, he would smile, continue on his way, and say nothing. All of us took it to mean that this matter was "...none of our concern..." as was his gentle custom of keeping certain elements of his life private.)

By Frater's own admission to me during one of our discussions, something—the details of which he causally disregarded with a wave of a hand gesture—happened that brought him back into the AMORC fold in 1955. The humor and glee with which he said this told me that the initial gesture of reconciliation was made by someone in the general leadership of the Order; something which placated Frater's feelings and soothed over his ruffled feathers, thus allowing him to make peace with the general leadership itself. It is my suspicion that whatever he learned from the Alchemist in Montana was added to by him through his own incessant work in the field. AMORC got wind of this, probably because someone there was the one who alerted Frater to this man's existence in the first place. But he insisted that he only allowed the wounds of the breach to heal in order for him to become more deeply involved with the Rose-Croix University and its developing program of Alchemy—a program he admired very much and wanted to influence—and to become involved with Orval Graves, whom he greatly respected and admired.

The matter of the relationship between Frater Albertus and AMORC does not end here as the reader now knows. For this was only the end of the first break between the Order and Frater. The second break would come later, and will be discussed shortly. However, I trust the reader will agree that we have established a relatively sound background against which we can now view Regardie, and how he came into the picture. Having done so, let us now turn our attention to him.

The year was 1954. But before we jump to that time, there are a few things the reader should know about the events that led up to the time of Regardie's involvement with the Rosicrucian Order, AMORC, and meeting Frater Albertus.

Regardie told me personally that he returned to his home in California from London, England, sometime in late 1946 or mid-1947, after having volunteered his blossoming psychotherapeutic skills to the US government in 1943, during World War II. It is not clear if he was actually inducted into any branch of the military proper, or if his role was that of a formally employed professional civilian who aided the war effort in this capacity. My own opinion is that the latter case is more probable from an impression I received when he explained this situation. (As with Frater Albertus, Regardie had his limits. He would not divulge certain aspects of his life to anyone.)

The US government stationed him in London, where he treated frontline troops suffering from shellshock and combat fatigue, who had been removed from battle due to their conditions. He worked there "for several years, both during and immediately after the war, rendering services at a well-known hospital in London's Imperial Quarter, near Piccadilly..." as he explained to me one night in 1979. While there, Regardie heard about AMORC from someone. Of course, this was not the first time he had heard of the "mysticism by mail order" organization that detractors of AMORC leveled against it in those days. But this time was different.

This time Regardie treated an American soldier who lived in San Jose, and who was a member of the order "...for quite a few years as I recall. This man impressed me considerably not simply with his knowledge of mysticism, but with his knowledge of Magic.

Israel Regardie & the Philosopher's Stone 51

He said he got his knowledge directly from the Rosicrucian Teachings! Need I say more?" he asked me. He continued,

"Don't forget, I had been through my Crowley days and the Hermes Temple of the Golden Dawn fiasco. I was still not over the first, and the second, well, it was the one real love of my life and I wanted to make it work at all costs. Eventually I wanted to see Golden Dawn Temples throughout America, so young people like yourself could come and study and practice Magic safely and sanely. But the war was on, and as I told you so many times, a man must do the task that is given to him at the time, and to the exclusion of all else! That's how a real man lives! All the rest just has to wait! And in my case, that was my own plan for the Golden Dawn and Alchemy.

"The same man I treated also told me that AMORC had a legitimate alchemy program, and that they planned to expand it after the war and make a real impact on this long-forgotten subject. It was so ideal I couldn't believe it! Here in one Order—the Rosicrucians—I had it all. If only the damn war were over, I thought. But as I said, I had to keep doing what I was doing at the time, and so let my beloved Golden Dawn and my dreams of Alchemy go for the moment. Oh, I also contacted some of the members of the Hermes Temple that were still around, when I had time off from hospital. But when I found out that one of the chaps from the Temple I told you about was killed in the Blitz on London, it took the starch out of me. There were some others, but by and large most of them dropped away from the Temple and went on into other things. So, I left it all go and continued to work. I contented myself by remembering all of those fools who posed as students of Magic in the Temple, how the Old Man treated me the years I was with him, and so I felt I was best off by having done what I did by publishing the Golden Dawn material. No matter what, I didn't want that material to disappear from the earth. At least that much was done.

"I would console myself with this new possibility with AMORC once the war ended. After all, it was a breath of fresh air as far as

Magic and Alchemy were concerned. I have to say that out of all the people I met in the Golden Dawn up to that time, this man from San Jose outshined them all like the sun outshines the moon! So, there was where my real hope lay back then."

I remember asking him some detailed questions about what he had just related to me. Such questions as,

"Did you contact AMORC immediately when you got back to the States? Did you join the Order? What was the Rosicrucian Order like back then? What did you learn? Did you get the Alchemy you wanted, and when did you meet Frater? Did they really teach Magic?"

But Regardie's steel-trap mind was as it always was. It followed a train of thought through to its conclusion, no matter what anyone else wanted. And to this day I owe him more than I can ever say for having instilled this same mental discipline in me. So, he continued.

"When I got back home, things were different. My practice—such as it was—had dried up. I was coming to learn of Reichian Psychotherapy and wanted to figure out a way I could practice it legally and safely so my future patients could benefit. You have to remember, that in 1947 I was forty years old. Not an old man, but not a young one either! So, it took years for me to acquire the credentials I needed by taking another degree at a small college not far from my home in Studio City, and combining it with chiropractic techniques so that I could practice 'manipulative treatment of the emotional disorders' as the State medical association allowed me to say and do.

"But learning more about Wilhelm Reich and his taboo ideas of psychotherapy and the Orgone Energy was not easy back then, and was even dangerous. Remember, he died in the Lewisburg Federal Penitentiary in your own state of Pennsylvania, for refusing to retract his views. Not to mention that his books were publicly burned by the federal government in the 1950s as well! It also took quite a bit of money to have the proper tools needed to practice such manipulative therapy. Like the special tables for the patients to lay on, and the orgone energy devices. All of this meant I had to keep my nose to the grindstone for years to bring it all about! Then too, as I said, a man must do the task that is given to him at the time, and to the exclusion of all else! And so I did.

"Oh, I kept my hand in things—at least in my own mind—by planning on writing more books while studying the Golden Dawn more deeply, and starting to revise some of my earlier books such as The Art of True Healing *and* A Garden of Pomegranates. But I didn't get around to actually revising the first until 1964, and didn't like the second one so much but I said to hell with it and let it stand as it was. However, by and large, I just kept doing what I had to do to establish a thriving practice in what I enjoyed so much, which is psychotherapy.

"But by 1954 I was seeing daylight at the end of my professional tunnel as it were. I was forty-seven years old then, and started to feel like a real success in life. And I certainly was, and from more than a professional, medical prospective too. My early books were becoming well known, some publishers [their names withheld for obvious reasons] were courting me, and as a result, more and more people were becoming aware of Israel Regardie of the Golden Dawn. I was feeling very good about myself and my life in those days. The burden I had placed myself under, that of becoming a success in the world and on my own terms, was becoming a reality so much so with each passing day, that I began to relax somewhat. And as I relaxed, more and more memories of the past began to surface.

"One of them was my memory of that soldier I treated in London all those years ago, and they began to emerge and reoccur very vividly. Finally, in November 1954, I decided to do something about it. I went out to a newsstand and bought a copy of *FATE* magazine. And sure enough, there on the back cover as usual, was a full-page ad for the Rosicrucian Order! I began to feel the same level of excitement I did all those years ago when I treated that soldier in London. I raced home, filled the coupon out, and remember purposely going out again to mail it. I couldn't wait for my letter of acceptance, and to start the lessons! Imagine, I thought, back to Magic, and real lab alchemy thrown on top for good measure! I tried to put it out of my mind, but with each passing day my excitement grew. Finally, three weeks later, I received a letter from AMORC. In those days they even had raised letterheads on the envelope and paper! I was so excited when I tore that envelope open..., and then everything came crashing down on me. I was rejected for membership, no reason given.

"I was so stunned I couldn't believe it. I just couldn't think. No one disclosed their memberships of such things in those days, so I didn't have any members to contact so I could ask why I was rejected! After I got myself back together, I called AMORC a few days later and asked to speak to the membership secretary. All I was told was that the decision to admit a person was a committee decision, and no further information could be given. I was no longer crushed, but so infuriated I cursed them out, threw the letter away, and vowed never to have anything to do with those people again! How could that soldier have steered me so wrong? At least, Joe, those were my thoughts back then. I just couldn't think straight I was that upset.

"Some months passed, and the memory of that soldier came up again. I wrote his name and address down in a small pocket notebook I used to carry with me in those days, but had lost it long since. Try as I might I couldn't remember his name. All I could remember was that he lived in San Jose. So, I gave up on the matter, and returned to my private life.

"Then in the summer of 1956 I had a patient who told me by way of conversation that he was a member of AMORC for the past six years, and that his life had turned around by applying their Teachings. He came to me because he had some childhood fears that still nagged at him, and wondered if they could be removed so he could continue his mystical studies undisturbed by the influence the resurfacing fears were having on him. I tried to find out from him if it was true that they really taught Magic and Alchemy. He would discuss neither in any detail due to the oath he took, but said that yes, they taught both, and that they were teaching Alchemy from the book Paracelsus himself wrote, which was the famous A.E. Waite edition!

"I knew of Waite of course, and while I thought he was an old stick in the mud, there was no doubt that his translation and literary abilities were first rate, especially prior to 1910 when he finally returned to Catholic views. That was enough for me. In a flash I knew what I had to do, and did it. Using my same mailing address as before, I applied to AMORC again, but this time under a fictitious name. I figured my reputation from my books may have preceded me the first time I applied and was so rudely rejected. I was right. This time I was accepted on the basis of the general, phony information I gave on the application.

"There were no problems at all, just a very friendly 'Welcome New Member' letter, addressing me as Frater Francis. So, I paid my $2.50 a month dues I think it was, and for over a year I studied their system. I never got to any magic right away because of all their Portal, Secret Mandamus, and Neophyte Degrees, but I found the mysticism very intriguing. The more I studied, the more I came to believe that they did not teach any Magic as you and I would understand it, but that their approach to Mysticism was not only mystical, but that it had magical overtones and that's why my new patient thought they actually taught it as well as Mysticism and Alchemy.

"I really enjoyed their lessons. They were very well balanced and so complete, I couldn't believe it. All in one place I was able to learn what I had to learn in patchwork fashion throughout the previous years. And that said a lot! So, I did get a great deal from it. I inquired about the alchemy outfit they were supposed to be selling, but found out it was no longer available. So, I was stuck. The supply bureau would only tell me that a new kit was coming soon, but just when, they didn't know. So, I put it off again and just continued with my Temple Degree studies.

"To be frank with you, from the time I came back to the States after the war until, oh, about 1963, I really didn't do any magic on any regular basis at all. I was tired and fed up with all the Golden Dawn stuff, the few people I knew who were still in it, and the others who were Crowley followers. Oh, Grady McMurtry and his bunch were nice enough in their way and all that, and for a while I did become involved with them. But now I was around fifty years old, and looking through the older eyes of experience. So much self-delusion and hoping. It made me very sad to think of those things again.

"I think it was in the Fall of 1957 that I again called AMORC about the alchemy. Why, I still don't know. So many years had passed since that soldier in London got me so excited about the subject again. So much had happened. But I called anyway. This time, instead of the supply bureau, I called around their offices and was finally sent to a Librarian. [I'm assuming Regardie actually spoke to Orval Graves, who was the Librarian at the time and who was Frater Albertus' early Teacher in Alchemy, as we know.] The Librarian told me that there was one, Albert R. Riedel, who '...has been working with me the past few years in order to expand the Rose-Croix University. We want to expand the classes by setting up extended alchemical classes of instruction at the Rose-Croix University. I'll be happy to take your name and let you know more as things develop.'

"Here I was, looking for an alchemy kit, and they had classes in alchemy that I knew nothing about! And after all of my telephone *calls! You would think that someone there would have known enough to tell me that such existed and that it was part of their very organizational fabric! But not one did. No one of the office bureaucrats apparently knew anything about it, and I had to find out for myself—after losing years in the process! I was beside myself!*

"*A few months later I called again, and made it a point to speak only to the same Librarian who helped me before. I had not heard from him, and was getting anxious about his silence. This time I made it a point to ask when Albert would be there. [Regardie always referred to Frater Albertus as Albert outside of class.] I also asked the Librarian if I could meet him [the Librarian] to discuss taking their alchemy classes. But he flat out said to me that '...if you were looking to enter the classes as they are now, before we expand them, you will have to speak with Frater Albert [later to become Frater Albertus] directly.' He told me that '...while I taught Frater Albert years ago, things have changed [probably as a result of Frater having studied under the mysterious Alchemist in Montana, who he found out about in the first place while taking the classes at the Rose-Croix University]. Frater Albert is now the one making changes to the course of alchemical instruction, and it is he who is handling the new admissions.'*

"*The Librarian went on to say, 'I am handling the administrative end now, at least that part of the process dealing with the administration which will make the alchemical instruction expansion possible and which will finally establish it as a major part of the Rosicrucian Order's duties and offerings to its membership.' So effectively, Albert was now the whole practical and teaching alchemical show at AMORC!*

"*I asked again if and when I could meet with Albert, and how to go about it. The Librarian took my name and telephone number again, and said he would pass it on to Frater Albert the next time he saw him. He also told me Frater Albert was a very busy man, and due to the expansion and some reorganization going on in the*

Order, he was now in San Jose for 2 to 3 days a week only. [Clearly this is a reference to Frater staying in San Jose for the alchemical classes he taught, and then returning to his home in Salt Lake City, Utah. This commute between the two cities would allow him to take care of matters both at home and at the Rose-Croix University.]

"Weeks passed, and no word. I remember it was in February 1958. I still had not heard from either the Librarian or Albert. So, I decided to take the bull by the horns. I drove to San Jose, got a hotel room for a few days, and just hung around the Order's grounds near the building they called the Rose-Croix University. On the second day I saw a large, very distinguished looking man with wavy blonde hair walking from the museum to a shed that was off to the side of the other buildings. He was in such a hurry, I figured it had to be Albert. So, I hailed him. He stopped, I caught up with him, and introduced myself.

"I decided to use my real name and not the phony one I had used to get into the Order. I figured, if the jig's up, it's up, because I couldn't continue going on the way I was. No sooner did I say my name before he took my right hand in those two giant paws of his and shook it so enthusiastically my teeth rattled! Before, my reputation damned me with AMORC. This time, it rescued me."

(This was Frater's early views on Magic and magical studies. Quite obviously, he had high regard for this occult field of study and experimentation, as he related to Regardie. His views on it and those who practiced it soured and quickly, over what happened between him and Regardie over the next several months. In fact, it was one case in which Frater blindsided himself, in my opinion. He was not prone to either generally or flippantly throwing the baby out with the bath water. In this one single instance however, he did just that. Those events and Frater's motivations for this will also be covered later on in this chapter.)

Israel Regardie & the Philosopher's Stone

"He told me he not only knew about my books and background with Crowley, but that he had heard of my deep interest in Alchemy from 'someone you do not know.' I didn't know what he meant by this, but I didn't care. I finally met the man I had waited so long to see."

It was, to coin a phrase, love at first sight for both of them. (Frater frequently alluded to the fact that he was privy to information he obtained from or through occult methods and techniques. From my own personal experience with him, I can most emphatically state that such events did happen, and that they were true. The Lesser Banishing Ritual of the Pentagram that Curt and I performed in our dorm room at the PRS that night is only one example. I have personally witnessed dozens more that came from Frater. And always, they were true and bore much fruit.)

Then Regardie told me how he and Frater spent the next two evenings together, discussing Magic and Alchemy. Frater surprised Regardie by the depth and breadth of his magical knowledge; something he is certainly not remembered for today. But during that two-day private meeting, he succeeded in impressing Regardie with his magical insights; and Regardie succeeded in impressing Frater with his almost desperate desire and devotion to learn and do laboratory work at any cost. Each man thought he had found his perfect double: the one who not only complimented those unexpressed elements deep within the nature of each man, but who would enable each to develop and manifest those elements as well.

By the time the two men parted that week, each was filled with joy and anticipation that all of us have known at different times in our lives: the joy of newness and possibility. And through the gateways, an expectation of their desires being fulfilled. The two shared an early relationship that had much of the flavor of that depicted between the main characters in Frater's later book, *The Alchemist of the Rocky Mountains*.

But, there were problems even at the outset. Namely, Frater was only spending 2 to 3 days in San Jose, **every other week**, not every week as Regardie had come to believe from his conversations with the Librarian! And even when Frater was in San Jose, Regardie would be separated from him by the 300-mile distance that stretched between the two cities! So realistically, how could Regardie learn the alchemy that Frater *had* taught at the Rose-Croix University? I say, had taught, because during the transition period to the new, expanded program of alchemical study, classes were suspended from operation. (It is important to remember that there were only two men who were struggling to bring the new alchemical program into AMORC existence: the Librarian, Orval Graves, and Albert R. Riedel. I should also note here that I have seen Frater's legal name spelled Reidel. Indeed, I even saw him spell it both ways myself. When I asked why, he gave his characteristic smile and made no answer.)

But they came up with an answer to the problems, and one that worked very well for Regardie. From June through August of 1958, Regardie took three, one-week vacations from his therapeutic practice and headed for San Jose. There, at the rather scanty facilities for alchemical experimentation set up at the Rose-Croix University, Frater taught Regardie all that he could about the Vegetable Kingdom of Nature (or the 'Herbal Kingdom' which is more accurate) as well as the rudiments of the work with metals, *i.e.,* the basics of the Mineral Kingdom of Nature.

But Regardie was not very impressed. He told me that three things became very clear to him as he worked with Frater in the alchemical laboratory:

1. While Frater was insistent that all phases of work in the Herbal Kingdom of Nature were thoroughly understood and experimented with in order to produce the Herbal Stone, Frater had not yet succeeded in producing one himself. (The Herbal Stone is a solidified, physical mass that contains—in proper proportion—the Three Alchemical Essentials: the alchemical Salt, Sulphur, and Mercury of a given herb. To produce such a 'stone,' the alchemist—***after gain-***

ing sufficient experience in manipulating the Three Alchemical Essentials through the Three Alchemical Processes of Separation, Purification, and Cohobation—puts an initial quantity of raw herb—usually five to 20 pounds of raw, dry herb depending on the nature of the herb being experimented with—through the Three Alchemical Processes until the Salts becomes so fused with the Sulfur and Mercury that a new, living material is formed: the Herbal Stone. When quantities of other raw herbs are then exposed to the Herbal Stone, the stone literally separates the alchemical Salt, Sulfur, and Mercury from them, such that they can be scooped up with a spoon and ingested by the alchemist. The theory behind this is that the concentrated essences of an herb which are 'extracted' by the stone give the alchemist the concentrated occult virtues and medicinal qualities that are ascribed to the herb in question. This product, the Herbal Stone, is what alchemists refer to as the "Little Work," and which is said in the literature of alchemy to give one "The Keys to working in the Kingdom of Metals," whereby one can proceed to produce the "Stone of the Wise," also known as the "Philosopher's Stone." The Philosopher's Stone is said not only to transmute base metals into gold, but to confer physical immortality to the alchemist who ingests it according to a prescribed procedure. Thus, Frater was absolutely adamant that all major efforts be directed by the aspiring alchemist to produce such a permanent, functioning, Herbal Stone.) The fact that Frater had not yet produced the stone of the "Little Work" himself, even after the instruction he received from the mysterious alchemist in Montana, while still lecturing about it and other herbal matters at AMORC, disturbed Regardie greatly. Yet he could not deny the physical benefits that he received from taking the "Herbal Tinctures of the Seven Planets of the Ancients" which Frater had instructed him in by the Three Alchemical Processes of Separation, Purification, and Cohobation. Consequently, by the end of July of 1958, Regardie determined that he would "…take it as far as I could with Albert so I could learn all he had to teach about herbs and the alchemy that applied to them. Ok, so he didn't make the Herbal Stone yet. That was bad, but I knew he was on his way and would succeed. So, I accepted things the way they were."

2. This business of Frater teaching work in the "Mineral Kingdom" as he called it through working with antimony, and his speculations on how to work with it safely, made Regardie very nervous. As Regardie told me,

"...well, it [Frater Albertus' teaching and working with antimony] just seemed like such a dangerous a thing to me. Especially since I felt that Albert didn't really know what he was doing when it came to something that contained arsenic! We both got our eyes and throats burned more than once when working with the damn stuff, and I was upset! Yes, I admit, I thought to myself, well, he doesn't know what he was doing yet, but knowing him as I do, he soon will. But that didn't mean I was going to be the one that would test that antimony tincture out for him!"

3. Because Frater had 'partial' knowledge of the Herbal and Mineral Kingdoms of Nature, and yet was making statements that Regardie took to be out of line with a broader experience, Regardie had determined by the end of July he would see the work through until the end of August. By then, as Frater had told him, "he '...would have all that I taught in the Rose-Croix classes. When the expanded program begins, then you can come here to study and get the advanced material...'" "What advanced material?!" Regardie complained to me, as if talking to himself that night. "Albert wanted to start the advanced classes at the Rose-Croix in the Spring of 1959, which was only eight or nine months away, and clearly, he needed to develop more on his own before he could teach from experience and not from speculation!"

Israel Regardie & the Philosopher's Stone 63

As Regardie explained to me, a rift occurred between him and Frater Albertus in mid-August, but over what exactly, he wouldn't say. The two reconciled quickly however, and by the end of August 1958, Regardie completed all of the instruction which Frater—and therefore the Rose-Croix University—had to offer at that time. But their parting left Regardie both cautious and upset as to what was going to happen next. For as he told me, all along Frater was

"making side comments to me that got me wondering. I have to tell you I got the impression that this new, expanded four-year program Albert wanted to institute at the Rose-Croix would contain no small amount of meditative and mystical techniques aimed at stimulating the student's spiritual development so the results in the laboratory could occur."

(It is a working model in Practical Laboratory Alchemy that the alchemical processes written down in the ancient manuscripts will only materialize in the lab when the alchemist achieves a level of spiritual unfoldment, as I term it, that is required of a given operation, whatever that operation may be. That is, Alchemy is both an Art and a Science. A spiritual art, in that unfoldment must occur which will then enable the science part of the practice—the chemistry part if you will—to materialize as the physical result being sought in the lab work.) Regardie went on to relate,

"And what is more, I felt he had targeted me to be the one to give those instructions. He was particularly interested in the Middle Pillar Ritual, and wanted me to consider adapting it to '...taking care of the spiritual component of the Work...' I put it off at first, because I just wanted to learn all he had to teach. Of course, I gave it no more thought, because I had a very good therapeutic practice back in Los Angeles even then, my life was there, and I certainly wasn't about to scrap it all and move to San Jose for any reason! Not for Albert or anyone else! But on that late August day when we parted, he brought it up again in a left-handed way. I said little or

nothing as I recall, but just let the matter rest there. Still, it left me wondering and somehow concerned as I returned to Los Angeles."

Soon after their parting, the fat got thrown into the fire. In October of 1958, Frater showed up on Regardie's doorstep. According to Regardie, when he opened the door, Frater burst in and told Regardie he had to speak to him immediately, and all but ordered Regardie to get rid of his patients for that day so they could talk privately. Stunned, Regardie told me he didn't know what to do at first. But his gentle way prevailed. He explained to Frater that he could not simply cancel his patients' appointments, and asked Frater if he would come back in the evening when he would be free to discuss whatever he liked. Frater eventually agreed, and returned at the appointed time. It was then that their relationship fell apart. As Regardie stated to me,

*"Albert was livid! He said that at some level the bigwigs of AMORC had made a decision. They had decided that the alchemy program would not only **not** be expanded as the Order had already committed to, but that it would either remain as it was, teaching plant [or Herbal] alchemy on a practical laboratory basis with a theoretical study only of the works on metals [The Mineral Kingdom] **or** that the alchemical teaching program of the Rose-Croix University would be dropped altogether. However, they had not made up their minds yet!*

"Not only this, but even their famed Alchemical Laboratory kit that they sold, and which contained advanced instructions that he and others had prepared, would be curtailed as well. Even the furnace that was an integral part of the kit would be left out, thus reducing the kit to, as he called it, '...a senseless collection of herbs and test tubes for idiots!'

"Then Albert told me that not only had he proposed a four-year expansion to their program, but since he and I last saw each other in August he realized that it would take a seven-year cycle program

to do all that was required, and so he introduced this second proposal to AMORC in September [of 1958]. At first, they were very keen on the idea, and agreed with him that such an expansion was necessary. Further, they wanted him to develop the program, while he was developing his own skills and testing his own insights in the advanced work on the Herbal Stone and on antimony. All was set, and even the funding was in place.

"Then, as he said, 'Two days ago, Israel [he always addressed Regardie in this way until the early 1970s after which he called him Francis], the Chief Administrator called me in and told me about this new decision! No explanation, no details, nothing. I was beside myself, and knew there was nothing I could do or say that would change his mind, and so told them I was done with him and his 'Order' and never wanted to hear from him or his organization again! I cleaned out my things from my office at the Rose-Croix University, have it all packed in my truck outside, and I am going back to Salt Lake City. Are you ready to come with me? Together we can establish our own institution. One that will teach alchemy and mysticism the way it should be taught, and without interference from fools who are only interested in their own profit!'

"I couldn't believe my ears! I mean, I knew what he was aiming at all along. You know, to move to San Jose and teach mysticism and meditative techniques! But to be asked outright, not to go there, but to move to another state! I told him I could never do such a thing. My practice was here, my life was here, and I enjoyed the warmth and pleasant weather California had to offer. I told him my license to practice 'manipulative treatment of the emotional disorders' was for California, not Utah, and that I was not about to go through all of that again to try to get a license to do my type of psychotherapy in another state! In fact, I told him, the Mormons who owned—not just ran—that state would never hear of it! Not to mention having to re-establish a practice that was now on the verge of thriving very well! But Albert would have none of it!

"He told me he knew people in the state department of education, and that we would have no problem getting my license transferred to Utah. He was not asking, if you know what I mean. Now he was ordering me to do this, and I had had enough! We came to some very bitter words, and I told him to leave. He did. And so, our relationship ended at that point. Little did I know it would pick up again a few years later, but that's how it went that day."

I trust that now the reader has some understanding of the series of historical events which unfolded and produced the men that both Regardie and Frater Albertus were, at least, how they were when it came to the pursuit of Alchemy. On the one hand, it satiated Regardie's desire to have assurance that there was indeed a physical and practical basis for what he had come to love and dream about throughout the decades: Alchemy. On the other hand, it shows how Frater Albertus received much of his hitherto unknown early alchemical training, and his relationship with that august body known as the Rosicrucian Order, AMORC, as well as their involvement in this strange and fascinating field of the Occult. It also conveys some other insights as well. Namely, the source from which Albert Richard Riedel took his final fraternal pseudonym, Frater Albertus. For as you now know, at the Rose-Croix University he was referred to as Frater Albert. But after parting with AMORC, he Latinized the name to Frater Albert*us*. That is, since he was quickly becoming a force in the world of Alchemy and Mysticism through his affiliation with, and the extensive work he had done with AMORC, he did not want to lose the momentum of that growing reputation. Hence his decision to Latinize his name. In addition, we can see how and where the idea for the Seven Year Cycle of classes of alchemical instruction came from, as this seven-year cycle idea would constitute the practical laboratory program of instruction at the famous, Paracelsus Research Society. This came from Frater's work at the Rose-Croix University and his attempt to expand their program of alchemical instruction.

Israel Regardie & the Philosopher's Stone

Additionally, and in my opinion—and that is all it is, *my* opinion—Frater's extremely negative attitude toward Magic of any kind, which lasted throughout the years to follow, was a reaction against what he saw as Regardie's betrayal by his refusal to move to Salt Lake City and handle the mystical and contemplative part of the soon to be Paracelsus Research Society program of alchemy and personal development. For indeed, as Regardie later explained to me in greater detail, Frater wanted Regardie to handle the morning classes in mysticism and contemplation, teaching the Middle Pillar Ritual among other exercises, along with adding whatever Golden Dawn material to the lectures that Regardie thought appropriate. Frater would handle the afternoon sessions in the laboratories, in which he taught not only the praxis but the theory behind the alchemical operations as well. Thus, Frater never overcame his fury at Regardie's refusal to assist him, even though the two would link up again in future years.

Upon returning from San Jose, Frater Albertus assembled a small number of individuals who lived in or near Salt Lake City. Throughout the following year, these few visited him "…several times a week…" as he stated. He went on to explain,

"It was during that year [1959] that we made the most progress. For during that one, single year, not only did I discover the keys to unlocking the production of the Herbal Stone, but also the keys to working confidently and effectively in mineral alchemy.

"In fact, it was during that year that the few of us working together in my small laboratory at my residence produced the first Unfixed and Fixed Tinctures of Antimony from the Glass of Antimony, as well as producing the Red and Yellow Kermes, and expanding immediately afterward into the work on lead in order to find the Green Lion, the Philosophical Mercury, the Red and the White Mercuries, and eventually, work towards the Great Stone itself—the Stone of the Philosophers."

Having succeeded at last to fulfill his own self-directed requirements, the man known to the world as Albert Richard Riedel, and to those in the Occult community as Frater Albertus, would formally open the Paracelsus Research Society (PRS) in the following year, 1960. These accomplishments also explain the famed *Alchemical Laboratory Bulletins* that were written and published by Frater from 1960 to 1972. It takes only a cursory glance at their content—even the content of the earliest of these bulletins—to realize the enormous strides in alchemical knowledge and ***experience*** that somehow came together within him during that 'Annus Mirabilis' (Year of Miracles) in 1959.

The history of the PRS—as well as Regardie's further interaction and my later involvement with Frater Albertus and this alchemical school of practical learning and work—will be given in the chapters to follow.

Chapter Three

The Alchemic Art Brought Down to Earth

The Organization and Formation of the Paracelsus Research Society

By his own admission, Regardie still had a very bad taste in his mouth over the confrontation that had occurred between him and Frater Albertus. Since that confrontation, he kept busy with his therapeutic practice, prepared the outlines for several more books he was considering writing, and stayed "...somewhat in touch with a few upcoming and promising Golden Dawn Temples here in the States..." He also devoted time to furthering his understanding of plant alchemy (which will be discussed in Chapter Four). But he had no knowledge of what Frater Albertus and his few students had achieved the previous year. Nor did he know about the formal organization that had been founded and launched in 1960, The Paracelsus Research Society (PRS). By the end of 1961 he would hear of the PRS, and as he commented to me one night many years later, "...at the time, I wondered if I had done the right thing after all by not at least exploring the waters that Albert proposed..."

To understand the events that are to follow, I feel a seeming digression will serve the reader best. When a historical accounting, such as the one being presented here, is being offered, it is always best if the reader acquires a flavor of the physical place where critical actions and events of that historical accounting occurred. To accomplish this, I propose to convey a layout of the physical area of the PRS, so one may be better able to get a feeling for the ebb and flow of the activities experienced in the seven yearly two-week classes, in addition to gaining an appreciation for the enormity of the will of its creator. In this way, the reader should be able to gain an emotional appreciation for the history that was made there.

While it is true that what is presented in this chapter are the perfected results of the PRS compound and the class activities as I experienced them during my 1975 to 1980 Seven Year Cycle (the third and last of Three, Seven Year Class Cycles), still, the insights gained can only serve to make the experience of Regardie, Frater Albertus, and the PRS, that much more meaningful and real. If studied carefully, the contents of this chapter should broaden the horizon of the reader so much, that one may think themselves an actual participant of those classes. At least, this is my intention.

But there is more. Owing to the complexity of some alchemical issues that will be dealt with later, I feel an introduction to those matters is necessary. For clearly, this book will be read by both the alchemical worker as well as the newcomer, and as much information as can be presented here should be given so both types of readers can be satisfied. For instance, I have written about the Herbal Stone and have provided some indication as to its physical characteristics and alchemical effects. Certainly more explanation would aid the newcomer. Likewise, in Chapters Seven and Eight, we will deal with the 'Generation of Animals' and the Homunculus. Such topics cannot have too much explanation, even for the seasoned alchemical worker. Then too, I have discussed the work on antimony with which Frater struggled in his early days, and which will eventually be found to play an important role in Regardie's alchemical efforts.

To cover these issues in what I feel is an eclectically balanced way, I am presenting below a paper I wrote on these matters in

Israel Regardie & the Philosopher's Stone 71

December of 2001, but which enjoyed only a very limited circulation. This paper, *The Alchemical Teachings of Frater Albertus and the Paracelsus Research Society,* should fulfill these requirements. I have edited the paper, only in so far as correcting some grammatical and syntactical errors; errors that were not caught prior to its original presentation. Otherwise, it remains as it was first written, even though some repetition and even ambiguity of what has already been discussed may surface. My reason for choosing not to edit it extensively is quite simple: history is always multifaceted to say the least, and different interpretations for any given action or event are always possible. Additionally, it has been my experience that repetition is not only one of the keys to learning; it is one of the fundamental keys to discovery as well. And that, my dear reader, is what Alchemy is all about—discovery—both of one's own Interior Realm, and of the alchemical results in the laboratory. Thus, the text below is the primarily unaltered form of the paper. There is also a "Suggested Reading" list at the end of this paper, one that in my estimation, should be placed here, and not in a "Recommended Reading" list at the end of this book, owing to its immediate relevance of the material presented in the paper.

I trust the inclusion of this work here will accomplish what it is intended to accomplish, and thereby lead the reader into a deeper understanding of the PRS, and the players who gave it the reputation it still enjoys to this day.

The Alchemical Teachings of Frater Albertus and the Paracelsus Research Society
(Reprinted here from the author's notes)

In October of 1980, I completed the seven-year in-residence classes of theoretical and practical laboratory instruction in Alchemy given by Frater Albertus, the owner and director of the Paracelsus

Research Society (PRS). From that time to this, I have not seen any tribute paid to this modern-day alchemist. Nothing has appeared in print concerning either the Society or his alchemical and alchemistical teachings. Conversely, over the past twenty-one years, I have heard rumors of the most shocking and disgusting kind regarding this man, his morals, the 'real' purpose behind his chemical and physical laboratories, and even of the layout of the PRS compound setting. Most of these ravings were (and still are) malicious delusions generated by those who neither attended his classes nor knew him personally. Others were propagated by some of his own students who were simply too lazy to do the interior self-examination and laboratory work he laid out, and who blamed him for their lack of results. I make this statement because I knew a number of those individuals personally.

Despite this occult mainstream nonsense, several of Frater Albertus' books remain in print to this day, for example, *The Alchemist's Handbook*, *The Seven Rays of the QBL*, *Praxis Spagyrica Philosophica*, and the collection of *Golden Manuscripts*, the latter of which he edited and republished in the late 1970s. Unfortunately, with his passing in July of 1984, the bulk of what he built—the entire PRS facility—has faded away. The buildings that served as dormitories and laboratories have since been converted into apartments. Other parts of the property were sold off to the highest bidder, while his vast library of alchemical research manuscripts dating back to the 12th century, were sold to book/antiquarian dealers, or discarded into the trash heap. Only his Alchemical Teachings remain; and those in the minds and laboratory journals of that handful of students to whom he orally delivered [tape recorders were not allowed] those teachings during those incredibly intense, yearly, two-week class sessions [and some teaching prior to 1960 and after 1980]—and those who did the ***work***!

Upon Frater's passing, and immediately before his own death in March 1985, my mentor, Israel Regardie, made the express statement to me that he wished the works of the man and the Society be remembered. In keeping with Regardie's wish and my own desire to once and for all quell the rumor mill, I have finally set down this curious paper. It contains the *facts* of the man and the PRS, based upon my eleven years of personal involvement with Frater Albertus. That period covers the time I was a student at the PRS and the years that followed the completion of those in-residence studies, right up to the day of his death.

These are the qualifications from which I desire to shed some light on the man and mage who chose to refer to himself simply as Frater Albertus—Brother Albert. And if, after having labored in the Art and Science that is Practical Laboratory Alchemy since 1974, I am fortunate enough in accurately conveying something of his instructions in attaining to alchemical transformations and transmutations in the physical laboratory —"Where it counts," as Brother Albert insisted, "where there is no place or room for the confusion and delusion that abounds in the realms of 'spiritual alchemy' and 'soul transformation' "—then the record will be set straight here, once and for all.

Frater Albertus was the fraternal pseudonym chosen by Dr. Albert Richard Riedel, a German national who came to America in the 1930s. As he personally related to one of my classes, he emigrated to escape the forthcoming nightmare he foresaw with the rise of Nazism. Prior to emigrating to America, he married Emmy in 1932. Without "Sister Emmy" and her tireless efforts to keep the dormitories and the students in order, it is very doubtful that he would have succeeded in his mission of bringing Alchemy down into the laboratory—where it belongs.

While Frater spoke fluent English, he nevertheless had a very slight accent which he disguised by speaking slowly and with perfect clarity. Even in his later years, "Frater," as we simply called him during our classes, was a large man, standing about six-feet one-inch. His broad, thick frame carried a heavily built body. His features were typically German for the time: a large face with well-proportioned ears, classical Roman nose, broad mouth, large, deep set blue eyes, and almost completely grayed-over blond hair. He was an imposing figure for any time period. And with his mental acuity and powerful logical faculty, he could have chosen any profession he cared to. His mastery of the scientific method was better than many scientists of my own profession of physics, while his analytical abilities were second to none. Yet, he chose to devote his life to teaching Alchemy, or "Parachemistry" as he preferred to call it, to those individuals he selected to attend the classes he taught at his research institute, the Paracelsus Research Society.

PRS was located at 3555 South 700 East, in an outlying county district of Salt Lake City, Utah. He chose this site to build his home and research institute due to the general climate and snow-capped Rocky Mountains that surround the city. All reminded him of the region of Germany from which he came. This residential setting allowed for peace and quiet during the periods of instruction, with virtually no interference posed by the distant neighbors that flanked the compound on three sides.

The compound was situated upon a substantial tract of land. It housed seven buildings: Frater and Soror's large, private home guarded by two enormous steel gates that bore the crests of the Red and Green Alchemical Lions; the two-story main dormitory; a research laboratory; a small, single-story home used to house European researchers and their families who came for extended periods; a second single-story home that was permanently occupied by two elderly relatives of Frater's and Soror's; and two single-level supplementary dormitories at the back of the property. The main dormitory had two fully equipped kitchens, one upstairs and one downstairs. It had four bedrooms downstairs and two on the second level, with two students per room. Each of the supplementary dormitories housed two to three students each, while the single-story home served the needs of up to four people.

In 1974 I was twenty-five years of age. Dr. Francis Israel Regardie, my mentor in Magic, introduced me to Frater Albertus in October of that year. Owing to my majoring in physics at university, Regardie considered it absolutely necessary that someone in the hard sciences be taught the ancient Art and Science of Laboratory Alchemy. Both Albertus and Regardie insisted that Alchemy be studied scientifically, and eventually brought into the light of the physical and chemical sciences, proper. But this, only after the peculiarities of this early science were understood on their own terms, and their claims evaluated objectively. In keeping with their aims and my own desire, I was admitted to the cycle of seven-year classes in February 1975. I completed the seven years in six years, by taking the fifth- and sixth-year classes back-to-back.

Separate application to each yearly class had to be made. That is, acceptance for one class did not guarantee acceptance into the next year's class. Typically, re-acceptance was based upon each student taking the instructions for a given class back home, and continuing that work in their own home laboratory. Each one had to bring their results back to PRS the following year, and demonstrate what they had accomplished on their own. This was a three-day period Frater designated as Show-and-Tell. If—as in most cases—a student neglected to do any at-home work for a year or two, he or she eliminated themselves by not reapplying for the following year's class. In some cases, those who did not actively pursue the experimental work on their own still applied for further instruction. They were denied subsequent re-admission outright. There were also some individuals whom Frater allowed to return for several years, even though they staunchly refused to do the required at-home laboratory work. It was his way of allowing the genuine spiritual transformation that occurs from even an acquaintance with Laboratory Alchemy to take hold, and point those aspirants into other directions that were more suited to their personality structure.

At some point in the seven-year program, these students also eliminated themselves.

At the opposite end of this student spectrum, individuals were admitted who could neither pay the nominal sum for the mandatory dormitory stay, nor buy their own food. In these cases, Frater waived their dormitory fee. He then gave them money to buy their own groceries and personal toiletries. This was done on one condition: that this money was never repaid to him, or to the Society. Rather, he requested that they do the same for another individual at some time in the future if their circumstances allowed. He told us many times, "When you come here for these classes, all of your needs will be tended to, whether you can afford them or not. This is done so you can devote yourselves completely to the work at hand." Such was the mundane component of this man's philosophy.

Each yearly class of the seven-year cycle was given a corresponding Latin designation: *Prima, Secunda, Tertia, Quarta, Quinta, Sexta,* and *Septa.* Generally, there was one complete, seven-year cycle of classes held at PRS each year from early February through mid-May. From early September through late October, additional Quarta, Quinta, Sexta, and Septa classes were held for advanced students from America, Europe, and Australia, who were unable to attend them earlier in the year. In the summer months, Brother Albert and Sister Emmy traveled to Switzerland and Australia on a yearly, rotating basis, where he taught students who were unable to travel to Utah. This schedule was maintained from 1960 through 1980, the time when Frater declared that our Septa Class was the final class of the seven-year class cycle. "The Twenty-One Year Cycle has been completed," he told us on October 31, 1980, the last day of Septa Class. [Update: In an *Essentia* article, Frater Albertus gives the PRS a birth date of December 28, 1959, and wishes it a 'Happy 21 year Birthday' for December 28, 1980.] "Yours is the final class of the Cycle." From 1981 throughout 1983, the classes were reduced to a Three-Year

Cycle, with a Fourth Year being attempted in 1983. When I asked him why, he smiled and replied, "Don't you know? My Work here is nearly completed!" He passed away in July 1984.

Each class had between twelve and twenty-one students. As the dormitories were fully equipped with daily living accommodations, it was not necessary to leave the compound, except to buy groceries for the upcoming week. Living at PRS for the two-week classes was mandatory. No one was allowed to take hotel or motel accommodations elsewhere. Nor were local students allowed to live at home during the class period. This encouraged full, around-the-clock participation by each student in the experimental laboratory work that began on the third day of class and lasted until the eleventh day. On the twelfth day, all experimental setups had to be torn down, laboratory reports written and submitted to him, and the labs and dormitories cleaned and prepared for the next incoming class.

The first-year class, Prima, was not simply devoted to the basics of Alchemy, but to Frater's teaching a **complete** curriculum of Occult Philosophy, but one which was 'template-like' in structure only, and which had to be adjusted by the individual to his particular circumstances. But more of this later. The philosophy that underlay this template however, was aimed at achieving a single purpose: the unique discovery and awareness of the Self by each student through answering three basic questions:

- Where did I come from?
- Why am I here? or, Why am I who I am?
- Where will I be? or, What will happen to me after this life?

To answer these questions, he taught the principles of Astrology and Western Qabalah individually, and then wedded them by an oral esoteric teaching in such a way, that by *applying* the principles, the first-year student began to experience the Self. Glimpses of the whisperings of Self and glimpses of the "I" forever changed the individual. But the astrology was not a coffee table type; nor was it exclusively that which is found in any elementary textbook on the subject. Rather, the "Astro-Cyclic Pulsations," as he called his astrological lectures, stressed the periodic nature and esoteric principles that lay behind the subject.

Each student was also required to carefully copy and color the numerous astrological and qabalistic charts and diagrams he presented to the class, as they embodied Frater's esoteric system of self-analysis and unfoldment. This mechanical procedure he insisted, would aid in the mundane understanding of the principles, while facilitating an unconscious absorption of them. Together, the oral teachings and the individual personal effort produce an effect that would eventually bring about a change or transformation in the spiritual nature of the student. This change, in turn, would allow the student to successfully work in the practical laboratory phase of alchemy. "Know thyself!" were among his special watchwords which he tried to instill in all of us.

The alchemical teachings in that first-year class dealt with the revelation of the physical nature and recondite qualities of the Three Alchemical Essentials as they are termed in the ancient alchemical texts: the Salt, Sulfur and Mercury; and of the Three Alchemical Processes: Separation, Purification, and Cohobation (to cohabit; to lie together). These were then applied to the most elementary Kingdom of nature: the "Vegetable" or "Herbal Kingdom." As he explained, the process of laboratory alchemy must begin with the application of the alchemical principles to this elementary realm of nature. For it was only by understanding how the Salt, Sulfur, and Mercury of an herb could be extracted through ordinary chemical means, and then recombined through the three processes of separation, purification and cohobation to yield a new creation that lies beyond the province of nature, that the student could aspire toward applying his or her knowledge of the three essentials and the three processes to the highest of the Three Kingdoms. This would be the Mineral Kingdom, that area of experimentation in which such compounds as the Philosophical Mercury, the Potable Gold, and the Philosopher's Stone itself, could be obtained.

Nor was it enough to be able to produce a simple alchemical tincture of a given herb, although to do so was to produce a powerful medicament for healing the body and balancing the mind. Rather, since the ultimate aim of *laboratory alchemy* is to produce the famed compounds mentioned, the student was encouraged to first learn how the three essentials and three processes are combined *consciously* in the laboratory to produce the **Herbal Stone**: a "stone" which not only mimics the virtues of the reported Philosopher's Stone, but which—through its production—teaches the student *exactly* those physical laboratory operations and esoteric principles needed to produce the *summum bonum*: the Stone of the Wise itself. Thus, the manipulations and principles to which the ancient texts only allude as being necessary for producing the Great Stone, are actually taught to the student through the successful production of the Herbal Stone.

It was the duty of each first-year student to take the processes of separation, purification, and cohobation as demonstrated in the PRS laboratories back home, and produce a set of "Tinctures of the Seven Planets of the Ancients" for his or her own use. This was done by selecting seven herbs, one that corresponded to each of the seven planets recognized in classical astrology. Each was then put through the first two alchemical processes to remove its salt, sulfur, and mercury. These alchemical essentials were then recombined through cohobation. The seven powerful tinctures that resulted were then imbibed over the course of the year. By doing so, gross material was removed safely from the student's physical body, while the qabalistic qualities of the planets were infused into the student's nature, thus preparing the individual for the advanced alchemical work to follow over the remaining six years of classes. It was also expected that each student would begin his or her own laboratory work on the Herbal Stone at home; a process that Frater cautioned, *"would take at least several years to complete. Nature does not give up her secrets easily! Nor does that realm beyond Nature, which will enable you to eventually succeed in this 'Little Work,' as the Herbal Stone is called in the literature."*

But what of these Three Alchemical Essentials? Just what are they? Do they actually possess a physical nature and occult properties? Are they the same in each of the Three Kingdoms of Nature? If not, how do they differ? And how are the Three Alchemical Processes applied to them? It is not possible in a paper of this length to give very detailed information regarding the above. However, what is given here is the **true essence** of the Three Alchemical Essentials and the Three Alchemical Processes. This, albeit brief, instruction will nevertheless enable the earnest seeker after the hidden knowledge of alchemy to **read the classical medieval texts with great profit, and will open up the kingdom of this ancient art and science** to his or her own experimental investigation—if the following is studied closely.

As Brother Albert explained in the Prima Class, the alchemical 'Salt' is the **body of the herb, animal, or mineral**. It is that which is left after the natural form has been reduced to its essentials by **Fire**. This 'body' is the same in all Three Kingdoms of Nature. That is, a substance with salt-like qualities and appearance, and whose chemical nature is **basic**, not acidic. It is the product of final reduction. It will undergo a change-of-state as it is purified—one that reflects the Supernal Triad on the Tree of Life. That is, it will pass through the color changes from black, to gray, to white—passing from Binah to Chokmah to Kether—as it attains purity. This is not only true of the Salt in the Vegetable Kingdom, but of the Salts in the Animal and Mineral Kingdoms as well. When it reaches the final stage of white, it can defy physical laws as we know them. An example being, the purified salt can literally rise up from the surface upon which it is undergoing purification, and float in the air. I have personally witnessed this a number of times, and have satisfied myself that air or thermal currents from the heating-purification operation have nothing to do with this phenomenon.

The alchemical 'Mercury' is the esoteric *Life* of the substance being worked with. It has different 'vehicles' depending upon the Kingdom of Nature in which the individual is working. In the Vegetable (Herbal) Kingdom, the vehicle of the Life is an *alcohol*. It is obtained directly from the herb being worked on by the technique of fermentation, and extracted by simple train-distillation. In the Animal Kingdom, the vehicle is the *blood*. In the Mineral Kingdom, it is an *alkahest*, and is removed from the mineral, *e.g.*, antimony, by first subjecting the mineral to a sub-process of Separation called digestion. In this step, a menstruum, or other liquid medium capable of binding with the alkahest, is first added to the mineral. In the case of antimony, the menstruum remains combined with the alkahest for use. The menstruum used with antimony to achieve this is common 190 Proof grain alcohol. This is used in preparing the Unfixed Tincture of Antimony. For producing the Fixed Tincture of Antimony, the *previously prepared* antimony is 'treated' with 6 N acetic acid to 'fix' its Mercury. The resulting antimonious acetate is then extracted using grain alcohol to separate the antimony's Sulfur and Mercury for use.

In the case of lead when the 'Great Work' is attempted, the menstruum is removed from the alkahest, after digestion, by another Separation—repeated distillations, the first of which is through simple train-distillation. The remaining distillations are only accomplished through laborious distillations using extremely exotic glassware that must be specially designed by the student and blown by a master glassblower.

The alchemical Sulfur is the *occult Consciousness* of the substance under investigation. In all Three Kingdoms of Nature, its vehicle is an *oil*. That is, a physical substance whose common qualities of viscosity, odor, and appearance resemble that of an oil. In the Herbal Kingdom of Nature, due to the minute quantities present, the oil is separated by the ordinary chemical process of dry distillation. Normally, many pounds of the fresh herb must be treated in this manner due to the exceedingly minute quantities of oil present in herbs in general. *The Sulfur is removed prior to the fermentation.* In the Animal Kingdom, the sulfur is obtained from the *yoke*, that part of the embryo which produces the veins, arteries, and blood of the animal. This Sulfur is extracted through an ether, soxhlet separation, a process that is actually easier than it sounds. In the Mineral Kingdom, the Sulfur is obtained from the alkahest, as it is bound with it by nature. This latter separation is not exceptionally difficult with, *e.g.*, antimony. It is extraordinarily difficult when working with lead.

As to the preparation of the Herbal Stone, or, accomplishing the "Little Work." After the student selects the herb to work with, it must first be dry distilled as stated earlier in order to obtain the alchemical Sulfur (Consciousness) of the herb (Separation). Following this, it is fermented to produce an alcohol, which is actually a 'wine' of the herb which will contain the alchemical Mercury—the Life of the herb (Separation). This alcohol must then be separated by successive train-distillations to obtain the pure alcohol of the herb. After the Sulfur and Mercury are obtained—and *according to their natural proportions as established by Nature*—the herb, now referred to as the 'feces' of the herb, must be incinerated to reduce its gross body (Purification). The first color achieved here is that of black (corresponding to Binah). In this state, the black ash is referred to as the *Caput Mortem* or, Death's Head.

Following this, the black ash is placed in an unglazed earthenware dish and calcined (varying degrees of heat being applied with a Fisher burner), to further reduce its mass by separating the essential from the nonessential parts of its physical nature. An unglazed dish is used to allow the ashes to breathe as the heat of reduction is applied. That is, air flow will occur from the bottom of the dish propelled by the flame beneath, and move *through* the pores in the dish, completely removing that which is unessential in the process. This is a very important consideration.

As the calcinations proceed, the black ash will turn to a dark gray, and finally—after approximately seven days of continuous calcination—to a light gray (a correspondence to Chokmah). The purification is continued for weeks or months—day and night—until the salts appear as a white, powder-like substance in the dish. These are the true alchemical Salts of the herb. Their essential Quintessence has a color and occult correspondence to Kether.

The beginning of the Little Work proper now commences. It must be remembered, as Frater Albertus stressed to us in class, the creation of the Herbal Stone is not simply a product of mechanical manipulations as employed in an ordinary chemical laboratory. Rather, since the Stone's creation is said to reflect the state of a genuine, not imagined, spiritual unfoldment of the student, success will only be obtained when the inner process of growth and the outer manipulations in the laboratory have achieved harmony. Hence the reason that it may possibly take years to produce.

The pure white Salts are now placed in a "Pelican's belly," as the medieval texts refer to a ***retort***, and the slow process of imbibition with the Mercury (alcohol) and the Sulfur (oil) begun. Drop by drop, the Sulfur and Mercury are added to the white salts until the salts take on the color hue of the Sulfur, and a semi-viscous mass results. This mass is left to cohobate ("lie together") in the retort, until a distillate appears in the arm of the retort. When the clear distillate reaches the lip of the retort, it is collected and saved. This highly volatile liquid is referred to as the ***"Sharpened Mercury of the Stone."*** The process of imbibition continues over months, until the semi-viscous mass cannot accept any more fresh Sulfur-Mercury combination. As the mass congeals and nears its endpoint by refusing to accept additional fresh Sulfur and Mercury, the worker must swirl the retort. As this is done, the mass will roll into a stone-like object. Now the final process of imbibition begins.

The Sharpened Mercury of the Stone is now applied to the hardened mass in the retort, drop by drop, over weeks or months. (Or if another of the several processes used to make the Stone is used, this process of adding the Sharpened Mercury is done during the 'fusing' operation.) The small 'stone' in the retort will now accept this more volatile Mercury. At some point the stone will refuse to accept anymore, evidenced by an even more highly volatile clear liquid being given off by the stone, and condensing in the arm of the retort. At this point, it is necessary to smash the retort to remove the stone-like object.

Finally, the object is placed in a glazed crucible, and Fire applied in ever-increasing degrees of temperature (the fusing operation) until the stone-like object hardens into what literally appears to the sight and touch as a real stone. I used a highly regulated, thermocouple-temperature sensing, solid-state *Blue M Muffle Furnace* in my own work. The temperatures used began at 100° C (Celsius), the work being completed at 1,000° C. While the stone is forming throughout the degrees of heat, it must be re-imbibed with the Sharpened Mercury after each treatment in the furnace. It is this final action that brings the stone to completion.

The finished Herbal Stone will be pure white in color, extremely hard, and extraordinarily heavy. The stone is tested by wrapping one end of an ordinary string around it, and attaching the other end of the string to a pencil. Several ounces of any dried herb are placed in a large glass vessel, *e.g.*, a 2-liter beaker, along with approximately 1.5 liters of plain tap water. After the herb becomes saturated with the water, it will of course, sink to the bottom of the vessel. The stone is then added to the beaker, such that it is suspended by the string-pencil combination at a point just below the water surface. What happens next is beyond the explanation of everyday science.

Depending upon the maturity of the stone, in a few minutes, the heavy, saturated mass of herb on the bottom on the beaker will float to the top of the water, and surround the stone. It will remain there for hours, after which it will sink back down to the bottom of the beaker. A few hours later it will float back to the surface again. This time, in only minutes, it will sink back to the bottom where it will remain. But floating on top of the water's surface will be found the entire Salt, Sulfur, and Mercury of the formerly dry herb. The Mercury-Salt-Sulfur combination is now simply spooned off and consumed by the worker as a powerful herbal medicament. In brief, the *action of a functioning, mature Herbal Stone, is to remove the Life, Consciousness, and Body of a raw herb and concentrate it in a very brief period of time.* The stone is then simply washed off and stored away for future use. It remains a permanent object, refusing to dissolve even in weak acids.

I should point out that there are several ways to make an Herbal Stone as mentioned above, all of which were discussed in detail at the PRS during subsequent class years. These other methods include making the stone from the light gray Salts as well, or from the water-soluble Salts that can be 'leached out' of the gray Salts. I have provided a few references at the end of this paper for those interested in pursuing this Work.

In my own case, I made four stones by four different methods, and demonstrated their action to Frater Albertus and my fellow students in my back-to-back Quinta-Sexta Class in 1979. It took four years of work to unlock that within myself which was necessary to create this alchemical material. The knowledge and experience of the alchemical procedures involved, and that which the final Herbal Stones 'conveyed' to me, are invaluable.

The next three years of classes, Secunda through Quarta, were concerned with working in the Mineral Kingdom of Nature. That is, expressly with antimony. Occurring in nature in the deadly form of antimony trisulfide, this mineral is always found bound up with arsenic. Frater explained to us that Nature hides its most precious medicines among its deadliest poisons. To unlock the secrets of the alchemy behind the laboratory operations, Frater gave each of us a copy of Waite's translation of *The Triumphal Chariot of Antimony*. Written by the German Benedictine Monk, Basillius Valentinus (Basil Valentine) in 1415, and first published in 1604 through the efforts of John Tholden Hessius (Johann Theolde), those three years of classes were spent going over the entire volume—literally, sentence-by-sentence, paragraph-by-paragraph, and page-by-page. Frater's initiated comments and further explanations along the way opened our eyes to the incalculable value of the manuscript before us.

From the Unfixed and Fixed Tinctures of Antimony made from the 'fume,' and the qabalistic colors of the Glass of Antimony this element produces when exposed to heats of 900° C to 1800° C, to the secrets of preparing the Kerkring Menstruum and the Sulfur of Antimony; to the final preparations of the "Butter of Antimony" and the methods of these compounds' safe, proper and natural use—all were covered in minute detail before their preparation was demonstrated for us by Frater in the laboratory. "Know the theory before attempting the praxis!" was his razor call before attempting any practical laboratory work in alchemy. As with each year's instruction, we took the knowledge we were given back to our homes and labored to reproduce the results on our own, prepared to show what we achieved during the next year's Show-and-Tell sessions. The reader would do well to remember, that if the explanations of the Three Alchemical Processes and the Three Alchemical Essentials are applied to *The Triumphal Chariot of Antimony* in a thoughtful way, the secrets laid out by Basil Valentine in that important work will open before his or her eyes.

In the fifth-year class, each of us was given separate laboratory space and all equipment needed. We were allowed to work for the two-week period on our own, reproducing or perfecting any of the antimonious marvels we had investigated in our home laboratories, and compare results with our fellow classmates. As with each class, extensive laboratory reports were prepared before the two-week period ended, and submitted to Frater for evaluation and permanent storage.

The curriculum for the final two classes, Sexta and Septa, was determined by Frater according to the makeup and complexion of the students who succeeded in completing the Seven Year Cycle. In some classes, work began on the "Green Lion"; others began their work on the "Philosophical Mercury," while others worked on the "Potable Gold." My class was instructed in what is reputed to be the darkest corner of alchemy: the "Water Work." It is a subject in which I was intensely interested, and which I spoke privately to Frater about in earlier years.

This work is based upon the theory and practice set down in *The Golden Chain of Homer*, a private manuscript translated from a Latin work circa the fourteenth century first into French and then into German. The English translation used was derived from the first German publication that appeared in Leipzig in 1723. It deals with the production of a substance termed "Gur," or the "Pre-Adamic Earth," from which the Three Kingdoms of Nature themselves can be generated. In other words, this is the primal base material from which all Creation arose. In the Christian-dominated Europe of the day, it is easy to see how this area of alchemical experimentation received the title of "Nature's darkest corner."

My interest lied solely in generating the Animal Kingdom of Nature. That is, to start with, the generation of small crustacean-like creatures Homer reported could be 'created' from simple rainwater, which was the foundational material of Homer's entire manuscript. What makes this work unique, is that this water must be collected during a violent electrical thunderstorm, following which it must undergo the process of "putrefaction" (chemical breakdown). The putrefaction produces the Gur, or Pre-Adamic Earth, which precipitates out of the water medium as a grayish, string-like substance. Following this, the experimentalist must obtain the "Water of Air, Water of Earth, Water of Water and Water of Fire," by successive distillations of the electrified and putrefied rainwater. These 'waters' are then used in certain combinations to imbibe the dried Gur. It is from this process that the creatures of the Animal Kingdom referred to above are generated. It is, as it were, an early experiment in Spontaneous Generation. However, the *Golden Chain* reports that the creatures generated do not fit any known species or genus. Approximately 200 gallons of rainwater of the type described are required to begin the process.

Our experimental efforts in this corner of alchemy were limited while at PRS, due to the putrefaction and distillation times required: six months to one year. But that work did begin, and the progress made demonstrated to us that there was indeed a basis in fact for what was written in the manuscript.

I continued the Water Work after completing the seven years of classes, and produced two papers which were published by Frater in his journal *Essentia: Journal of Evolutionary Thought in Action.* The first paper was entitled "The Analytical Technique Applied to the Water Work: A Modern Approach." It appeared in Volume 1, Winter 1980 issue. That essay dealt with the very real everyday problems encountered in collecting and handling such a massive quantity of rainwater. Modern techniques of 're-electrifying' the water and effectively putrefying and distilling it were also given, such that other contemporary workers could also delve into this alchemical branch of Nature's mysteries. These techniques were based upon my own successful efforts.

After two more years of work, my second paper, "On the Generation of Animals" was published in *Essentia,* Volume 3, Summer 1982. The cover of the journal featured a full-color photograph of the Gur-Water combination and the crustacean-like creature that was generated by the Homeric process. The paper itself, complete with numerous photographs, explained the process completely in everyday terms so others working in the field could reproduce the results for themselves. As stated by Homer, the crustaceans that resulted could not be classed into any species or genius when given to zoologists and biologists to identify.

Following these successes, Frater and I had several private discussions regarding what is traditionally described as the blackest area of this dark corner of alchemy: the creation of a "Homunculus." This was the single goal to which I directed my alchemical investigations after completing the seven years of PRS classes.

According to legend, this creature appears as a miniature human being. That is, it is made from the Salt, *i.e.*, possesses a physical body, which is infused with the Mercury, or Life itself. But it does not possess a Soul, or 'consciousness' in alchemical terms. It is up to the alchemist to work with such a creature, and give it a purpose to fulfill. The Salt for this Grand Experiment is the Gur, or Pre-Academic Earth. The 'Mother Earth' in this context is the Body. The Mercury or Life must come from the "Father." That is, from the alchemist himself. For in this particular realm of alchemy, only a male alchemist can generate the Homunculus, as his seed must impregnate the Mother Earth. After the impregnation occurs—as with a human child—the cycle of development and growth begins. The rest is left up to the reader to fathom—or to 'reproduce.'

In closing this paper, it is my sincere hope that the knowledge and instruction presented herein will serve to forever dispel the gross accusations and pseudo-intellectual diatribe leveled against the genius and man who was Frater Albertus—Dr. Albert Richard Riedel. He initiated understanding and love of knowledge and wisdom, and opened up the secret paths of Alchemy to hundreds, perhaps even thousands, of individuals throughout the world. *That work is **still** being carried on today in the private alchemical laboratories of those few of his students who persist in carrying out his highest axiom: "Work!"*

Suggested Reading

The following books, when used with the information provided in this paper, will help the desirous student to unlock the mysteries of the Three Kingdoms of Nature.

Frater Albertus. *The Alchemist's Handbook.* 1987. Weiser Books, York Beach, Maine. (At the time of this writing this work is still available. It will give the student specific knowledge on working successfully in the Vegetable (Herbal) Kingdom of Nature, and shed much light on modern-day chemical laboratory operations.)

Golden Manuscripts. With an introduction by Frater Albertus. Kessinger Publishing, LLC, Kila, Montana.

Basilius Valentinus. *The Triumphal Chariot of Antimony, with the Commentary of Theodore Kerckringius, A Doctor of Medicine.* Translated by A.E. Waite, Kessinger Publishing, LLC, Kila, Montana. (This book is also currently available from the cited publisher. Complete details on working in the Mineral Kingdom of Nature are contained within.)

H. Nintzel, compiler. *The Golden Chain of Homer.* 1723 edition. Restoration of Alchemical Manuscripts Society (RAMS), Richardson, Texas. (RAMS has ceased to exist. The rights to this and other alchemical manuscripts were turned over to the Rosicrucian Order AMORC, San Jose, California. At this time, the manuscript in question is available from them.)

Glauber, Valentine, et al. *A Compendium of Alchemical Processes.* Kessinger Publishing, LLC, Kila, Montana. (A very useful overview of processes directly involved in producing the Stone of the Wise.)

A.E. Waite, editor and compiler. *The Hermetic and Alchemical Writings of Paracelsus.* 1910 edition. Kessinger Publishing, LLC, Kila, Montana. (The "Great Book" of Alchemy, in both theory and practice. The essential one source for reference and working.)

Chapter Four

Israel Regardie & the Herbal Kingdom of Nature

Regardie related to me in the Fall of 1978,

"It was around November of 1961 I think, that one of my sources in the Golden Dawn told me he heard about a school of alchemy that had opened the year before. You have to realize, I had been on so many wild goose chases over the years in all these magical and occult matters that at first, I didn't pay much attention to the news. I had more than enough on my plate every day, and at the age of fifty-four back then, I was getting pretty fed up with the lot of it. Yes, things weren't as bad they are today, rumor-mill-wise, but still, they were bad enough as far as I was concerned. So, I dismissed the matter out of hand easily.

"But the following month near Christmas, a Catholic priest friend of mine brought up the subject while we were at dinner. He told me he had made contact with this new school of alchemy. He was very interested in alchemical work as well, and was studying [the alchemical writings of] Paracelsus, Glauber and Valentine for years, but never made much headway in his own experimental attempts to work with these things.

"For him, there were just too many unknowns in the underlying processes that defined the alchemical laboratory effort: symbolic phrases and verses meant to explain techniques and processes that he could not interpret; pictures and descriptions of vessels that were either mysterious or incomplete; a lack of precise instructions behind such key concepts as the 'Regulation of the Fire;' a lack of information regarding the degrees of heat; and hidden meanings in such admonitions as, 'Let the Eagle fly seven times...' that escaped him.

"Oh, I was polite at first when he started talking about this so-called school because as I said, I had heard about it from that other chap the month before. I've got to tell you that at that point in the game, my mind was closed on the matter. I was about to dismiss his comments until he told me this alchemy school was in Salt Lake City, Utah, and that he had contacted the Director of Studies there named Frater Albertus! You can believe me when I tell you that my mouth dropped open! I couldn't believe it. I began pressing him for all the details!

"He told me there was a seven-year program being offered at this new Paracelsus Research Society as it was called, not only in the theory behind herbal and mineral alchemy, as the Director explained to him, but in the laboratory practice of these things, and that each year's classes were two weeks long. He had very little housing for the few students he had been taking since early 1960, but since most of the ones he accepted were from the Salt Lake area it was not a problem. They just showed up every day for class and then went home for the night. The few others who came from greater distances he either managed to accommodate in a make-shift dormitory, or else they stayed at a small hotel nearby.

"I pressed him for more details on just what was taught, but he said he didn't know anymore at the moment. He did expect to receive a pamphlet from the school explaining its programs in more detail, but it had not arrived yet. I was crushed. It was very clear to me that Albert had gone and done what he said he would. He was very determined the last time we talked, I'll give him that, and yes, there wasn't a doubt in my mind even then that he would succeed and all that, but eventually! Not this soon!

"And here I was, working myself silly in my own homemade lab, devoting whatever time I could to this alchemy business. Making every conceivable medicinal herbal tincture under the sun to treat this complaint and that ailment. Testing all the claims he and the old [medieval] alchemists had made. Calcining alchemical salts day and night for months on end until they turned white. Having alcohol extracts catch fire more often than not. Ordering pounds of fresh herbs which I can tell you were as not easy to get back then as they are today. Doing dry distillations of the damn things [herbs] to get the volatile oils over first, and even trying my hand at making an Herbal Stone using what Albert knew about making it when we were together back in 1958.

"And now there he was, apparently having succeeded in unlocking the secrets of the Little Stone, and that for starters! I was sure of this, because during our row at my house that night he told me he was going to open his own Institute of Alchemy no matter what. But, he said he wouldn't do that until he had succeeded in the Little Work, and had made much further progress with antimony and even with lead! He was adamant about this! Now it was clear to me he had succeeded in all of it, including the antimony and the lead to boot!

"He taught me all he knew at the time at the Rose-Croix, but had apparently pulled out all the stops and somehow got to where he wanted to go! And as you know from having attended the classes, one thing is sure with Albert. He stands by his Word and does what he says he's going to do! Let me tell you, those GD [Golden Dawn] yahoos could learn a hell of a lot from him in this regard alone! And now there I was, on the outside looking in! I can't tell you how disgusted, angry, and utterly frustrated I was—not only at myself, but at him! Why the hell didn't he call me when all this came about? Why couldn't he bury the hatchet and all that, because we did get on well that summer we worked together! Didn't he see that I just *couldn't up and run, and drop my life in California? He didn't drop his in Salt Lake and move to San Jose for AMORC!"*

This is when Regardie made the statement to me that when he had been sitting at dinner with his priest friend during the Christmas season of 1961 he had wondered if he had done the right thing by not at least exploring the waters that Albert had proposed. But it was too late, the die had been cast.

Regardie continued to fume over the matter until February of 1962. It was apparent from his remarks and the manner in which he delivered them, that he wanted to blame Frater Albertus for everything, including his own refusal to even consider Frater's offer. Regardie then went on to explain,

"I knew Albert would not contact me. That damned German stubbornness of his prevented it. My Reichian work told me that he had too much body armor, especially in his trunk and chest area for him to ever admit he was wrong in insisting I drop everything and move to Salt Lake with him, and I was not even thinking the offer through more carefully. I'm certain I would have reached the same conclusion and taken the same actions that I did, but at least I would have felt justified now. Well, at least I think so. But with Albert, he wouldn't let himself see how wrong he was. His body armor and the neuroses and repressed emotions it hid wouldn't let him. So finally, I decided to write him a letter.

"I remember mailing it around mid-February. I waited. And I waited and waited. It was in early June of 1961, I think. The matter had me on the fence, off and on for months, until I finally forgot about it. Then suddenly around June I recalled it again, and realized that I received nothing as a result of my effort! Albert didn't even have the courtesy to reply to my almost self-humiliating letter! This set me off even more, since I was the one who made the first gesture at reconciliation! And damn, Albert had flung it in my face

by not so much as a reply? I was so outraged by his callousness that I finally picked up the bloody telephone and called him.

"I reached Emmy. We had never met up to that time. She was nice enough, but said that Frater was in class and would return my call later. I never expected to have that call returned. Why should he call? He didn't have the decency to accept my letter! Now I loathed him and the letter I sent, since it was just a blatant letter of apology. I should never have done that. But that night, very late, Albert called! He was as sweet and charming as could be, and spoke in that almost-singing, melodic voice he puts on. You know how infuriating he can be at times. He went on to swear up and down that he never received my letter, but had wondered about me throughout the past years. He told me he thought of getting in touch, but was reluctant to do so due to our unfortunate last meeting. I have to say, I believed him, and felt bad for assuming the worst about him.

"We had a very long and good discussion that night, that ended with his offer to place me in a class, starting with the fourth year Quarta! I told him about the extensive plant alchemy I had busied myself with since our parting, and all the progress I had made. I also told him I made numerous attempts to produce the Herbal Stone, by following his instructions at the Rose-Croix, but that I hadn't had any luck. Yet, I was concerned that if I entered the fourth-year class I would be completely lost, since I knew nothing about the work on minerals except what he taught me earlier, and I hadn't pursued it in my own laboratory.

"But Albert told me there was no problem with either of these things. He explained that in his 'First, Seven Year Cycle of Classes' [1960–1966] as he called it, the first three classes were devoted almost exclusively to working with herbs, since he was absolutely insistent that the class participants have the knowledge and some laboratory experience that would enable them to make the Herbal Stone while they were back at their homes for the year, between classes. *In the second year [Secunda Class] he began to phase in some theory on antimony from Basil Valentine's, The Triumphal Chariot of Antimony, and in the third year [Tertia Class] more of it to prepare the students to work with it in the laboratory during the Quarta Class.*

"Nevertheless, since he primarily stressed the herbal work during the first three years, and after my explaining to him all I had done in the Vegetable Kingdom, he said I was ready to start the work on antimony, and could pick up what I needed on plant work in that fourth year class that would enable me to make the Little Stone later, on my own time, at home. I eagerly accepted his invitation for the Quarta Class, which he told me would be October of that year. Then he dropped the bombshell. He apologized for any misunderstanding and said that the soonest he could 'allow' me to come would be in April of next year since the October class was filled. I was livid! This was Albert getting back at me, and I knew it! He didn't change one bit! But I swallowed my anger and pride, and asked him to send me the paperwork for the April class. At long last I was on the verge of getting the knowledge and practical experience in both Herbal and Mineral Alchemy that I wanted, and that was all I cared about. So, I went to my first PRS Class—the Quarta Class—in April of 1962."

(Note: It is my understanding that with the founding of the PRS in 1960, Frater—in principle—was prepared to be able to offer all of the seven-year classes from the very start, and that he had been working with students prior to 1960. Therefore, in any given Seven Year Class Cycle, during *each* of those seven years, Frater taught several of Prima, Secunda, Tertia, Quarta, Quinta, Sexta, and Septa Classes. That is, each year was not simply devoted to a single yearly cycle class, such as Prima only.)

Ironically, as Regardie explained to me in a later conversation in 1979, he did not complete that first Seven Year Cycle of Classes by taking the Quarta, Quinta, Sexta, and Septa classes. He did finish the Quarta Class in 1962 and the Quinta Class in 1963. But for business and health reasons, he had to drop out of the remaining two classes at that point. Eventually he completed all the classes by taking the Prima, Secunda, and Tertia Classes during the Second Seven Year Cycle of 1967 through 1973. (Even though Regardie did a massive amount of work on his own between 1958 and 1961, and received what he needed to complete his Herbal Kingdom education during that first Quarta Class of 1962, he was unable to successfully produce the Herbal Stone. As a result of these failures, he formally took the Prima, Secunda and Tertia Classes during the Second Seven Year Cycle, thinking that the added knowledge and experience would enable him to succeed in the Little Work.)

Regardie went on to take the Sexta and Septa Classes during this Second Seven Year Cycle as well. Then he repeated the Quarta Class in the Third Seven Year Cycle (1974 to 1980) for his own reasons, skipped the Quinta, and repeated Sexta and Septa Classes during the Third Seven Year Cycle. Therefore, Regardie would be the only person I am aware of, who was present for classes in all three of the Seven Year Cycle of Classes. There were others who repeated some of the classes, but these people only did so during any given single Seven Year Cycle.

It is important the reader understands something at this juncture. Much of the perfectly linear class structure and teaching syllabus was not implemented until the Third Seven Year Cycle of Classes, 1974 to 1980, and even here, as will be explained below, it was subject to change. Indeed, according to Regardie who was present in all three of the Class Cycles, Frater's program underwent considerable revision and expansion for the first fourteen years, that is, between the years 1960 to 1973. The classes were not congruent. Lectures and experimental work that appeared in, for example, one Quarta Class in the First Seven Year Cycle did not necessarily appear in that same class during the Second Cycle. Further, the syllabus could even vary from class to class in any of the Cycles.

For example, the content of what was taught in the Tertia Classes held during the Spring of say, 1963, may have varied from what was taught during those same classes that were given during the Fall of that year. So, while they could be similar, topics and the amount of laboratory work could differ slightly. At other times, especially in the advanced classes from Quinta through Sexta, the material could be significantly different. For example. In my 1979 Sexta Class and 1980 Septa Class, we worked on the Water Work from *The Golden Chain of Homer*, exclusively, while other Sexta and Septa Classes of those same years worked on the Green Lion, the Philosophical Mercury, or performed further work with antimony. It all depended upon the personalities of the class, and upon the different experimental agendas Frater held as being important for that particular class and for himself.

Now, what of Regardie's extensive work in plant alchemy with which he busied himself after their angry parting in 1958? Exactly what did he do, and what progress did he make? And what of his numerous attempts to make the Herbal Stone during those early years, based on what Frater Albertus had taught him at the university? Regardie sent me many documents on these matters. These were originals he wanted me to keep for a later time. These documents gave his work in detail, but not his reasons for doing this work in the Herbal Kingdom of Nature. From our discussions throughout the following years, and from the documents he sent me later on in the early 1980s, I have reconstructed his work. The reader may not only find the following interesting from an alchemical point-of-view, but may even gain a deeper insight into the man, Regardie, and his intense passion to learn and succeed in Alchemy.

Early on in their Teacher/Student relationship at the Rose-Croix University, Frater Albertus introduced Regardie to what he considered to be the most important and valuable Herbals of our time, as Regardie put it. (And as far as I am concerned, they remain the most important Herbals extant; not only for Alchemy, but for any occult

Israel Regardie & the Philosopher's Stone　　　　　　　　99

work as well.) It was from these two Herbals, *A Modern Herbal*, by Mrs. M. Grieve and the original *Culpeper's Herbal*, that both Frater Albertus and Regardie extracted the necessary medicinal and astrological information they needed to work successfully in the realm of Herbal Alchemy.

In Grieve's two-volume, 1931 set, the synonyms, parts used, habitat, description, constituents, medicinal action and uses, dosages, other species information, preparation, uses, and special considerations (such as its use as an antidote) are given clearly and completely for hundreds of herbs. (The Dover Publications, 1971 unabridged edition is still available at the time of this writing.) When combined with the early seventeenth century *Culpeper's Herbal,* the full spectrum of a given plant's characteristics can be easily understood and employed with confidence.

Nicholas Culpeper, a famous astrologer/physician of the period, devoted much of his time studying not only medicine, but the astrology behind medicine, and he published a number of treatises on the subject. His crowning result, *Culpeper's Herbal,* not only provides such information as where to find an herb in question, but its flowering time, medicinal virtues, and modern uses, in addition to its astrology—that is, an assignment to one of the Seven Planets of the Ancients, thus awarding the alchemist or other occultist to be able to work with an herb for a specific purpose, and to do so knowledgeably and confidently.

(In 1983, *Culpeper's Color Herbal* appeared on the market. This new edition presents the original information with the addition of color to the hand drawings, making it very easy to identify herbs in the wild. I strongly recommend it, along with Grieve's two volume set. No other herbals are needed by the serious alchemist, magician, or occultist. At the time of this writing, this book also still available.)

Armed with these herbals, Regardie set to work in the small alchemical lab he had established in a tiny shed in his backyard in

1959. As Frater had taught him, his first task was to produce the "Tinctures of the Seven Planets." One tincture had to be prepared for each day of the week using an herb that was assigned to the planet ruling each of the seven days of the week. Thus, seven tinctures were prepared. One would use a plant said to be ruled by the Moon, for Monday, ruled by Mars for Tuesday, ascribed to the rule of Mercury for Wednesday, ruled by Jupiter for Thursday, under the government of Venus for Friday, under the dominion of Saturn for Saturday, and a plant that was under the auspices of the Sun for Sunday. These alchemical tinctures were said to remove gross, malformed or putrefied material from the body, thereby gradually returning one's body to a state of natural health. That is, these herbal, alchemical tinctures are said to remove such material from those organs and biological processes that are ruled by each of the Seven Planets of the Ancients.

After removal of this material, according to Frater Albertus, the Tinctures of the Seven Planets of the Ancients proceed to refine the physical nature of the individual further, thus enabling the spiritual nature to come through more powerfully than ever before. As a result, the individual's entire nature—physical, mental, emotional, and psychic—are purified and equilibrated, allowing one to more easily and completely manifest one's own will and the Will of God that flows through one's nature, into the world of form, or Malkuth. These tinctures are then to be "imbibed" on each day of the week over the course of an entire year. Thus, on every Monday of each of the fifty-two weeks in the year, the Tincture of the Moon is to be imbibed. On Tuesday, the Tincture of Mars. On Wednesday the Tincture of Mercury. On Thursday, the Tincture of Jupiter. On Friday, the Tincture of Venus. On Saturday, the Tincture of Saturn, and on the Lord's Day, the Tincture of Sol (the Sun). This is how the aspiring alchemist began his training under the guidance of Frater Albertus and his seven-year course of instruction at the PRS.

Regardie produced these Tinctures of the Seven Planets of the Ancients in 1959, and as he told me very candidly, was extremely happy that he did. Not only did they help to restore his waning physical vigor, but they eased and checked his chronic stomach, lung, and eye conditions, along with an intermittent bowel problem. (I too can attest to the virtue of these tinctures, having made and used them immediately after my Prima Class in 1975. They aided enormously in actually eliminating some lung and sinus problems I had for years, and which conventional medicine was utterly inept in relieving, let alone 'curing.')

But Regardie's lung condition was ongoing, and as he told me near his passing in March of 1985, he felt that even if the two alchemical accidents had not happened, his condition would have gotten progressively worse, and—as he said—would either be the cause of his demise, or would contribute to it significantly. (Later, as the reader will see, his lung condition did become very severe, but we can only *know* that the two alchemical accidents he had while working with the dangerous compound, antimony trisulfide, were the actual causal agents for his lung condition degenerating faster than expected.)

When Regardie set to work in 1959 to make these tinctures, he not only made seven as instructed, but an eighth as well, which was made to target his lung condition. Thus, while he used Fern to expel choleric and mucous from his stomach as the herb for the Tincture of Mercury for Wednesday, he used Fenugreek, another herb under Mercury to remove 'humors' from his chest and lungs. And they worked magnificently. He also used Adder's Tongue, ruled by Cancer and the Moon to alleviate his bowel problems as well, this herb being his choice for the Tincture of the Moon for Monday. His notes also show that he used Arssmart, under Mars, for his Tuesday Tincture, Dog's Grass for Jupiter, Golden Rod for Venus, Barley for Saturn, and Feverfew (corn) for the Sun.

To make the tinctures alchemical, required an application of basic techniques—somewhat modified and elementary in nature—of the Three Alchemical Processes that constitute a beginner's entrance into Alchemy. These are the (elementary) processes of Separation, Purification, and Cohobation, which were performed in the following manner, and which gave Regardie—and all those who follow the Teachings of Frater Albertus—the essential Tinctures of the Seven Planets.

Essentially, Regardie proceeded as follows, his procedures being one—*and only one*—of the possible ways to obtain the Tinctures of the Seven Planets. (In actuality, there are several versions of the processes to be described, ranging from the simple use of 190 proof ethyl alcohol—the type purchased at liquor stores for consumption—as the menstruum, to more complex techniques such as those used by Regardie, the different virtues of the more complex measures producing even 'sharper' tinctures.)

Regardie began by taking a predetermined quantity of the herb he selected for the tincture, and placed it into an appropriate glass vessel fitted with a cork—no rubber or plastic stoppers are allowed, due to the possibility of the tincture leaching the chemicals out of such items. Over this, he placed a menstruum, or 'extracting medium.' In Regardie's case, he used an alcohol derived from the grape, the ideal menstruum to be used when operating in the Herbal Kingdom of Nature, as Frater Albertus taught. Specifically, Regardie distilled the grape wine to obtain the alcohol. (Both Separation and Purification are achieved in this operation, the latter, owing to the extreme of making successive distillations, as the reader will see next.)

After obtaining the alcohol from the grape wine, he **distilled it six more times, for a total of seven distillations.** Hence the meaning of the alchemical phrase, **"Let the Eagle fly, seven times."** This menstruum—the alcohol—was then placed over the dried herb, the vessel corked, and the assembly placed in a sand bath at 85 degrees

Israel Regardie & the Philosopher's Stone 103

Fahrenheit where it was left to "macerate" for one to two weeks. (Separation occurs here as well, the alchemical Mercury and Sulphur being 'separated' from the herb by the menstruum at this point. Additionally, some water-soluble Salts are also inevitably picked up by the menstruum.) That is, during this time, the menstruum absorbed the Mercury (Life) of the herb—whose *vehicle* in the Herbal Kingdom of Nature is an alcohol—as well as the alchemical Sulfur (or consciousness) of the herb. Thus, during maceration, the clear alcohol takes on a characteristic color of the herb, indicating the alchemical sulfur—the consciousness of the herb—has commingled with the alchemical Mercury in the menstruum, the great majority of Salts being 'hidden' with the mass of saturated herb in the vessel.

Now, the menstruum is decanted, and the alcohol-saturated herb—also referred to as the "feces"—is ignited. This is the phase of Purification. It is left to burn until it turns black, which is the Binah phase of the operation. In this black state it is also referred to as the "Caput Mortem" or the Death's Head. This substance, the Caput Mortem, contains two types of alchemical Salts: the soluble or "fixed" Salts and the insoluble, or "water soluble" Salts. This black substance is then calcined usually for a day or two over the open flame of a Fisher burner until it passes through the color change to gray, the Chokmah phase of the operation of Purification. If the calcinations are continued for weeks or months, the Salts will eventually turn a pure, crystalline white, which represents the Kether phase of the operation with this additional Purification.

However, to begin using the alchemical tinctures immediately, the feces is typically calcined to a light gray only, and then added back to the colored menstruum. The vessel with its contents is placed back in the sand bath where the alchemical Salts, Sulfur, and Mercury "Cohobate," *i.e.,* 'lie together,' each affecting the other in a unique, occult way. (This process is also referred to as "Digestion," in which the alcohol—the vehicle for the alchemical Mercury—

assimilates or "digests" the Salts that are contained in the gray, calcined mass.)

The vessel is placed in the sand bath once again for approximately a week, the vessel being shaken several times a day to enable the menstruum to absorb the Salts. After the week of Cohobation (or Digestion) has been completed, the resulting tincture is strained through a piece of laboratory-grade filter paper. The now 'dead' gray mass is discarded, and the resulting tincture—complete with the alchemical Salt(s), Sulfur and Mercury of the herb, are placed into an appropriate cork-stoppered glass container for use. In Regardie's case—as in my own—a single teaspoon of each of the seven tinctures was taken each day for one year. Thus, on Monday, a teaspoon of the Tincture of the Moon, was imbibed; On Tuesday, a teaspoon of the Tincture of Mars was taken; on Wednesday, a Tincture of Mercury was ingested, and so on, throughout the course of an entire year. As Regardie told me,

"...it really amazed me. After taking Albert's tinctures for that year, all of my chronic conditions cleared up completely and stayed that way for three years. But afterwards, I had to make another batch and begin the process all over again. I did this a few times. But by the late 1970s I grew tired of it and scrapped the whole herbal thing. I was using the antimony tinctures since the late 1960s daily anyhow, and they did the trick very well. Still, I enjoyed using the herbal tinctures, so I made them a few times as I said, and as far as I can see, benefited from them quite a bit as well."

But Regardie did not stop there when it came to the Herbal Kingdom of Nature, even though he had run the gauntlet of preparing the alchemical tinctures of the Seven Planets of the Ancients in the laborious way most other students at the PRS classes avoided like the plague. From our discussions and his private notes which he sent me, it is clear he was fascinated by this, the 'simplest' of Nature's realms. For he continued macerating, distilling, calcining, cohobating, digesting, and performing all of the basic alchemical procedures over and over again, in different combinations, using various herbs throughout the years, testing the various qualities of herbs, and their effects upon him and some of his close friends. He also obtained the bituminous-like matter from which the alchemical "Salt of Salt" of an herb is obtained, and used it as the basis of his first attempt to make an herbal stone: an effort of Regardie's we will now take a look at in more detail.

From 1959 through 1967, Regardie experimented extensively with herbal alchemy. And even though he received what he needed in that Quarta Class of 1962 to make the Herbal Stone, and took the formal Prima Class in 1967 in which Frater Albertus gave extensive directions on succeeding in this task, somehow, producing a permanent, functioning stone escaped him. (Every Prima Class from 1967 on contained such extensive instructions on making the stone, from what I have been able to learn. Yet, of the hundreds of students who passed through the PRS doorways, only a very, very few were able to successfully produce this stone: that which gave the individual the 'Keys' to working successfully in the Mineral Kingdom of Nature, and hence the potential to make the Great Stone of the Philosophers.)

In 1968, according to what Regardie told me in 1980, and as his own laboratory notes from those years show, he "...began the Little Work in earnest. Even though I was so very serious about it, I have to tell you, that I always felt there was something lacking in me that just wouldn't allow me to succeed. Maybe Albert is right. Unless your spiritual nature is up to the job, you can perform all of the laboratory operations you want, and you'll get nothing. I have to say, I am damn well getting to believe it!" But for Regardie, it didn't end with this confession of his.

There was something else nagging at his soul when it came to working in the 'Higher Alchemy' of the Mineral Kingdom: the clear, clean unfoldment of the individual's spiritual nature, so that the energy and beauty of that Interior Realm could and would effect the alchemical processes conducted in the laboratory. It was as I wrote earlier: unless a person's spiritual nature 'unfolds'—not 'develops,' as the New Age crowd insists—there can be no success in practical alchemical laboratory work. Even in such a minor thing as preparing the Fixed Tincture of Antinomy from the powdered Glass of Antimony using 6 N (Normal) acetic acid to first produce the antimonious acetate. Unless the worker's spiritual nature has unfolded to a certain degree, not even the soxhlet extraction—a standard chemical (*not* alchemical) laboratory operation—will succeed in yielding up the antimonious acetate from which the marvelous Fixed Tincture is obtained.

I have witnessed this myself on several occasions at PRS, when someone using the same equipment I used; who took the Glass of Antinomy from the same batch I took mine; who used the same bottle of glacial acetic acid I was using and who made the 6 N dilution exactly as I had done; who took the extraction thimble from the same box I had taken mine, and who had the same rate of reflux. Yet all came to naught for them. While the flask of my soxhlet extractor and others was filled with an intense, reddish-brown antimonious acetate solution after only several hours of extraction, this person's extraction media—the acetic acid—was as clear and colorless as it was when the hotplate was first turned on to supply the heat for extraction.

It was just this occult or 'hidden' aspect of Alchemy that disturbed Regardie so greatly, since it tied in with his devotion, dedication, and insistence that the Golden Dawn—and hence the system of spiritual 'development' he believed it taught to those desiring to 'Climb the Tree of Life'—availed him nothing when attempting the Little Work. In some way—as all of us do at one time or another—Regardie was able to rationalize away this failure of the Golden Dawn System of Magic to influence his alchemical laboratory work. And he did it in such a way, that he then blamed

Frater Albertus for not teaching a "...complete, coherent system of Mystical growth that will enable anyone to work the processes correctly!" as he commented to me one evening in 1980. "He let us all down in this, and that includes, you too, even though you made those four Herbal Stones successfully," he said. He went on,

"Don't forget. If Albert would have taught some solid stuff in Mysticism, you might have gotten the results quicker and a heck of a lot easier than you did! I read your lab notebooks you sent me. You're either very dedicated or as crazy as Albert, because you went through a God-awful lot of work and expense for years to get those miserable little rocks."

Regardie was looking for a Mystical Path to follow, and one that would, if not replace his beloved Golden Dawn System of Magic, at least give him a parallel path by which he could bring about what he desired so greatly to bring about in alchemy, while yet clinging to his Golden Dawn System and those beliefs around which he had built his entire life. And since Frater Albertus did not supply the 'Instant Mysticism' that he craved, it left Regardie sour on this so-called failing of Frater's, and on his long-term opinion of Frater himself.

A seeming digression is necessary here, to tie the multifaceted aspects of what has been given so far in this chapter with what is to follow. That is, if it is to make sense. So, let us consider those elements that I feel are essential to this understanding.

The reader may well wonder why, if Frater Albertus taught a 'complete system of spiritual unfoldment' during the Prima Class from (at least) 1967 onward, Regardie—among so many, many others—did not find it fulfilling, applicable to them, or at the very least, somewhat practical. For such constituted Regardie's complaints to me about the mystically-oriented 'system' that Frater did indeed teach during every Prima Class. My answer to this, based upon my own experiences with Frater Albertus, and from working his 'system' myself, is as follows.

First of all, it took Frater Albertus time to develop such a mystical system. As is true for all of us, we do not become finished works overnight. Realistically, most of us require decades of consistent, diligent study and work to even see light at the end of our own tunnels. And even when we do see that Light, we require more time to reach it, and afterward, even more time, so we can become comfortable and justified in that Light, once we finally 'arrive.' Such was also true of the mystically-oriented system Frater taught in my Prima Class in 1975. And even then, it became clear to me right off that the Qabalah (not Kabbalah as I prefer) was of the New Age variety, while the "Astro-Cyclic Pulsations" (both Western as well as Hindu astrology) along with the general mystical ideas of Self and its relationship to God, were presented as a template only.

That is, each student was to study and work in the Inner Realm with the ideas Frater presented, extract (from each of the components of Frater's system of mysticism) what was applicable to the individual, place that extracted essence aside, work with the next component, extract its essence, place it aside, and continue on with the all of the other components of Frater's teachings until all were worked through carefully and completely. At long last, the student was then to take all of these extracted essences and weld them into a *personal system* that allowed one not simply to glimpse one's true nature—the Self—but in doing so, to Touch the Face of God, thereby becoming a whole and integrated human being as a result of the mystical transformation that such a 'touching' inevitably brings with it.

It matters not if such touching is called "Attaining to the Knowledge and Conversation of the Holy Guardian Angel" or "Coming to the Christ Consciousness" or "Touching the Face of God." What was at the heart of Frater's Mystical Teaching was uniting with Godhead, if even for the briefest of moments. In other words, to attain Cosmic Consciousness. Once achieved, the individual's spiritual nature unfolds so fully and powerfully, that indeed, a new man or woman and a new earth result.

It was not at all that Regardie did not understand these things, even though he pooh-poohed the idea openly to me, and throughout the years of our relationship. For during our first face-to-face meeting—which lasted the entire week of October 8th to the 15th, 1973—and which occurred at his home in Studio City, California, Regardie insisted that he never wrote any book entitled, *The Romance of Metaphysics*. Indeed, it was not until 2004—thirty-one years later—that C.S. Hyatt informed me that Regardie did indeed write such a book and in fact, it was originally published by Aries Press in 1946! I immediately obtained a copy from a used online bookstore, and read it through. Not only did it become abundantly clear to me that Regardie knew much, much more Mysticism—including New Thought, Christian Mysticism, the Unity School of Christianity Movement, etc., but that his failure to implement the mysticism which he understood so well, **was due to his inability—or more accurately, refusal—to 'Cross the Line' from Magic into Mysticism**. It was as simple as that.

His early relationship with Crowley; his bad experience with the Hermes Temple of the Golden Dawn; his varied experiences with Old System Magic; even his private and secret work with Spiritualism which he told me about in detail; all had somehow produced within him an inability or refusal to find any form of Mysticism that was acceptable to him. This, despite the very clear problems with the Golden System of Magic that was (and remains) so eclectically imbalanced, and which produces results that are anything but desirable for its devotees. In short, it was not Frater Albertus' failure to provide a workable system of Mysticism by which Regardie could obtain the necessary (further) spiritual unfoldment he needed to successfully work in Alchemy: it was Regardie's own failure to accept *any* mystical system, owing to his refusal to abandon Magic and move on to Mysticism.

This, then, is *my opinion* of what laid at the root of Regardie's alchemical problems. For as we shall see later on, he was quite talented in Alchemy, and in fact, was able to work in those areas of the Mineral Kingdom of Nature to be discussed later, while being very obviously barred from other areas owing to this lack of (further) spiritual unfoldment. The intense, complex, exceedingly time and energy demanding type of Mysticism which Frater Albertus taught during the Prima Class had nothing whatsoever to do with Regardie's fundamental problem. For those others who found this system too demanding, it was clearly due to their sheer laziness, demand for instant gratification and the quick fix, which prevented them from hammering out Frater's very doable form of Mysticism that would have eventually led them to that experience of Self Discovery that they mouthed was so important to them.

We can now return to the matter at hand, and see Regardie's efforts to produce the Herbal Stone.

From 1968 through 1979, Regardie did his best to produce the Herbal Stone. He learned of the various methods of its production, not only from Frater's instructions, but from a particular manuscript that Frater reissued in the late 1970s during my years at the PRS, and which was one of the now famous *Golden Manuscripts*. (Like Regardie, I purchased all of these five manuscripts—not four as appears in the Kessinger Publication version available today. However, Frater had made them available to both Regardie in 1968, and to myself in 1976, so we could get on with our work.)

Published by Frater through the PRS as small booklets of varying length, these beautifully gold-covered booklets not only opened up new avenues of alchemical investigation, they cleared up many obscure points in those alchemical processes we worked with daily while at the PRS. The one in particular that interested Regardie was *Circulatum Minus Urbigeranum, Or The Philosophical Elixir of*

Vegetables with the Three Certain Ways of Preparing It Fully and Clearly Set Forth in One and Thirty Aphorisms, by Baro Urbigerus, London, 1690. (In fact, the techniques taught in this single, small production enabled me to produce three of the four Herbal Stones I demonstrated to my classmates.)

Other methods of making the stone included the technique of producing it from the light gray Salts (derived from the calcinations of the Caput Mortem) as well as a stone made from water-soluble Salts that can be 'leached out' of the gray Salts, and from the "Salt of Salt" of an herb. In Regardie's case, the method he favored most and which he experimented with from 1968 through 1976, was that of using the Salt of Salt of an herb. In all cases of producing the Herbal Stone in the 'classical' manner, the Mercury of the raw herb must first be obtained. (There are expediencies that can be used here, such as using 190 Proof ethyl alcohol as a menstruum, instead of fermenting the herb and distilling over the alcohol produced by the fermentation. But the stones that result from such a process never mature, nor function in a complete manner. Hence, they are referred to as 'Non-Classical' or 'Contemporary' techniques, and will not be discussed in this book.) It was no different in this 'Salt of Salt' method that Regardie used. Indeed, this method is perhaps the most difficult and laborious method of all the classical methods.

Since the herb is fresh (or raw), the experimenter must first ferment the herb such that it produces an alcohol; for this alcohol will be the vehicle which contains the alchemical Mercury—the consciousness—of the herb. But it is not as simple as that. The student cannot simply throw some general yeast into a vat containing tap water, cover the vat, and allow the little yeast fellows to do their job! Not here. Not when dealing with techniques that are meant to give one the Keys to working successfully in the Mineral Kingdom of Nature. No. Here, the experimenter must learn—to a reasonable degree of proficiency—the art of the winemaker.

This 'simple' winemaking activity alone lends insight into certain processes and procedures that most certainly will be used in the Mineral Kingdom of Nature. Thus, for example, the correct type of yeast must be determined and calculations of the alcohol content must made in advance of the wine wished to be produced—usually no more than 17% by volume—so that the fermentation process can be controlled. One must: know how to stop or accelerate the fermentation *naturally*, and not by using some chemical expedient; obtain five-gallon (typical) food grade containers—or "fermentation vessels" as they are technically referred to in the art and are made especially for the home brewer of wine; know how to use bubble air locks, hydrometers, filtering systems, wine thermometers, siphoning and bottling equipment, to name a few of the materials and their correct usages one must learn to produce the proper alchemical vehicle that will contain the Mercury. And that is exactly what Regardie did. Painstakingly, over that torturous twelve-year period.

(Note: What follows concerning the production of the Herbal Stone from the "Salt of Salts" will have to be read many times, and carefully, especially by the newcomer to alchemy. While I have done my best to make the presentation as clear as possible, still, the nature of the process and the many individual steps that cannot be recounted here, can make the process very confusing if one has little or no laboratory experience in these things.)

Throughout the period 1968 through 1976, Regardie employed his favorite Salt of Salt method to try and obtain the stone. Specifically, after obtaining over twenty gallons of the wine of Rue— attributed to the Sun and Leo—from twenty-five pounds of the *fresh* herb, he distilled the entire twenty gallons of wine—500 ml (milliliters) at a time—until approximately two US quarts (1,893 ml) of pure, clear, volatile alcohol remained. Thus, the Mercury of Rue was obtained. After each of the 500 ml quantities were distilled, Regardie placed the larger quantity of residue that remained in the distillation flask aside. This process was repeated throughout each of the 150-plus distillations necessary to reduce the twenty gallons of Rue wine to the final 1,893 ml of the Mercury of Rue.

Now, the residue of each successive distillation left in the distillation flask was added to the initial quantity of residue taken from the first distillation. A large quantity—approximately seventy quarts—of this dark brown-black, liquid matter was *very* carefully distilled again, such that the first volatile one-quarter part that came over was placed aside as the Sulfur or consciousness of the herb, due to its oily nature. In the case of Rue—Ruta graveolens, also known as Garden Rue or German Rue—the volatile first-quarter part that comes over is a beautiful yellow-golden oil which contains the alchemical Sulfur, or consciousness, of Rue in its final phase. However, this first one-quarter part of the seventy quarts does not produce an equivalent of seventeen quarts of the oil! Oh, if only! After further separation by slow, retort distillation, Regardie wound up with approximately one hundred and fifty-five milliliters of the pure, golden Oil of Rue, containing the alchemical sulfur and hence the consciousness of the herb. This is how demanding and laborious this particular technique is. Thus, he had finally obtained the Mercury and Sulfur of Rue, directly from the fermentation products of the wine of the Rue.

But what of the Salts? Surely, shouldn't that twenty-five-pound mass of herb that produced the initial twenty gallons of Rue Wine contain the Salts? And all that had to be done was to calcine this 'feces' of the herb through the colors from black, to gray, to white, to obtain the Salts? Correct? No. Not in this case. For in this method, due to extraction of the alchemical sulfur directly from the residue from which the alcohol (Mercury) was initially obtained, the Salts undergo a "...transformation of sorts..." as Frater explained to us during my Prima Class. In this case, the "...heart of the Salts, the Salt of Salt, is contained but hidden in the distillate from which the Sulfur is obtained..." as he said.

Thus, Regardie took the remaining massive quantity of residue, distilled off the bulk of the liquid until he had obtained around 500 ml of the most bituminous-like, dark brown-black substance imaginable. When dried in a sand bath at 100 degrees Fahrenheit over a period of weeks, the final product—a black, brownish-tan mass with yellow striations in it—results. This mass, when calcined through the color phases, changes from black, to gray, to white, finally yielding the Salt of Salt used to make the stone. After these Salts are finally obtained, they are placed in a Pelican's Belly—a retort no larger than 250 ml volume (owing to vapor pressure considerations in the retort during the forthcoming distillation process), and the process of imbibition begins. During this process, the purified alcohol (Mercury) obtained from the distillation of the wine of rue, is added drop-wise to the Salt, as is the Oil of Rue (the Sulfur). The Salt-Mercury-Sulfur combination is left in the retort, in a sand bath with a temperature no greater than one hundred degrees Fahrenheit to cohobate. Finally, a pure distillate—the "Sharpened Mercury"—that comes over through the arm of the retort, is collected and saved for future use. This process of imbibition with Mercury and Sulphur continues over months, day and night, until the (now) stone-like matter in the retort will not accept any more of the Mercury-Sulfur combination. At this point, the retort is swirled until the mass takes on a circular shape, much like a small marble, or stone.

At this point, the retort is smashed, and the 'fusing' of the 'stone' begins. This is done by subjecting it to ever increasing degrees of heat. This 'Heat of Formation' as I term it, differs for each stone. Generally, however, I found that temperatures from 100 to 1,000 degrees Centigrade—not Fahrenheit—perform the required fusion quite well. (A muffle furnace, either gas-powered or electric, is used to bring about the fusion.) During the fusing process, the stone will become very dry and brittle, and reach the verge of cracking into small fragments. Great care must be used at this stage. For when this dryness occurs, the experimenter must then begin adding the Sharpened Mercury that was collected during the imbibition process, to further 'wet' the stone and give it the added Life that is being driven off through the fusing process. If all goes well, within a few more months, the final stone emerges, ready to perform those duties that were outlined earlier. If not, if something goes wrong along the way, the entire process must be started again. And this is what happened repeatedly to Regardie from 1968 through 1976. For some reason—during one point of the operation or another—something went terribly wrong, and he had to begin again. Throughout the twelve years of his attempt to produce the Herbal Stone by the Salt of Salt Method, he attempted it six times, but all to no avail.

In early 1977, as he explained to me, he gave up on the Salt of Salt Method, and from that year through late 1979, he attempted to produce the stone by another, 'easier' method, by attempting to obtain it from the water-soluble Salts. But again, all to no avail. Finally, in 1980, while he, Frater, and I were doing other alchemical work yet to be discussed here, Regardie told me that he was "…thoroughly fed up with the entire damn thing! How I only wish I had taken my education in physics or chemistry, or even astronomy! Then I would have the mind-type that I still think is necessary to succeed in alchemy, no matter what Albert says! But it's too late now, and so I am just going to go on with what we are doing." And this was another point of contention between Regardie and Frater Albertus. While the latter insisted that the elementary laboratory operations and equipment handling procedures could be learned by anyone, either on his own or by taking university courses in inorganic and organic chemistry, Regardie insisted that a certain type of 'physical thinking' was necessary for one to delve into the deepest and darkest corners of alchemy. My being a physicist may or may not have influenced Frater Albertus in choosing me to do certain work which we shall soon explore here. But for Regardie, it was not a question at all. For him, my being in the Hard Sciences was that which was required. And because of this, I truly feel to this day, that this was one of the reasons he not only gave me his time and instruction in magic and other matters, but his friendship as well.

Perhaps the reader now has a better understanding of the courage and absolute steadfast determination that characterized Francis Israel Regardie. Not only in his unswerving adherence to the Golden Dawn and the system of magic he clung to so staunchly, but in his exhaustive pursuit of alchemy as well. Although Regardie did not succeed in producing the Herbal Stone, he nevertheless went on to do very important work in the Mineral Kingdom of Nature, as we shall soon see.

Chapter Five

Israel Regardie & the Animal Kingdom of Nature & the Formation of the Trinity

In September of 1978 I completed my Quarta Class, and upon returning to my home in Pennsylvania, I was busy duplicating and extending the work on antimony that our class had engaged in while in Salt Lake City that year. But some other, more important events happened during that class as well. For it was during that class that my old friend and colleague, Hans Nintzel, discovered a rare manuscript in the 'closet depository' as we called it. This was a large closet on the second floor of the main dormitory that Frater used to store the overflow of ancient alchemical manuscripts he had assembled over the decades. And what an overflow it was!

When Hans showed me the document, *The Golden Chain of Homer,* I was never the same again. In it, the writer had outlined a method of artificially generating small worm-like or crustacean-like creatures from electrified rainwater, a close kin to the scientific work I was doing on the origin of life at the time, and which I am continuing to this very day. Beyond my immediate fascination with the Homeric process, I wondered if any part of it could be used to expand my own scientific work, bent on generating 'life in a test tube' as it were, which was akin to the Nobel Laureate, Dr. Stanley L. Miller's generation of amino acids—the basic building blocks of all life—by passing radio frequency electricity through a primordial reducing atmosphere in the early 1950s.

Hans made a copy of the *Golden Chain* for me while we were at class. It so happened that one evening while in the laboratory, Frater came in unexpectedly, saw I was reading the document, and asked if I was interested in this strange alchemical process. (He already knew about the scientific work I had done throughout the years along Dr. Miller's line of experimental inquiry.) Of course, in light of my own scientific experiments, I told him I was more than interested, but just couldn't find time to get around to the Homeric work. After all, I had to go back home to Pennsylvania and—as he required—duplicate the antimony work we were doing during our Quarta Class, and extend it into different colors of the Glass of Antimony, thereby preparing for the Quinta 'Show and Tell' for next year. He smiled, and told me,

"Yes, most certainly go on with your work on antimony. But I want you to study Homer carefully, and be prepared to give me as best a scientific analysis of it as you can for next year's Quinta Class, because you most certainly will be admitted to it. I think it important you know that this work may have some bearing on your own scientific investigation on the origin of life research, but if it does, it will not be much. At least, that is my opinion. But it will have even deeper and more grim implications for you as time goes on."

Since I didn't understand what he meant, I asked him,

"Exactly what do you mean, Frater? I don't like operating in a vacuum. If I'm going to spend time with the Homer thing when I could be advancing my other work in Alchemy or science, I don't think so. Because I have to tell you that this Homer is so plain in many ways and yet so cryptic in other ways, it's as if there are parts of it missing! But I can't tell, and don't want to get caught up in some incomplete work for some idealized alchemical reason! I mean, I have real work to do, and so many of these alchemical

Israel Regardie & the Philosopher's Stone

things seem to me like three sheets in the wind. It's interesting, sure, but I don't think I want to go any further with it at this point. Certainly, not experimentally as Homer suggests, because it asks for a lot of work with no clear outcome, except for supposedly 'generating' little bugs! I don't see of what value that can be to me!"

Frater sat down on a stool in front of me, smiled broadly, and began to elaborate.

"You know, Joe, how insistent I am on people making the Herbal Stone before they even think about delving into lead and kid themselves about making the Philosopher's Stone? How I preach and continually tell them that only through their mastery of the 'Little Work' can they come into possession of the 'Keys' that will permit success in the 'Great Work' in the Mineral Kingdom of Nature?" I answered in the affirmative because by that time, I had four years of his drilling this prerequisite into me.

"Well, imagine the same situation here. Imagine that this 'basic' work as outlined by Homer is preparatory to something much greater. Something very dark and yet, something so fascinating, that people like us cannot resist it. In fact, it constitutes the darkest area there is in all of Alchemy, and yet..."

He paused, and with a faraway look in his eyes, seemed to be talking to himself. In fact, I felt like a fly on the wall, watching this big man mumble things I didn't understand. Then he went on.

"And yet, that realm can teach us so much about our Creator, ourselves and our world, in addition to showing us the secrets of Life itself! Can you imagine such a thing? Can you tell me you are not interested in such a dark, and even 'diabolical' pursuit? That is, of course, how the world in general would think such a thing. Because most assuredly, that is how the world has seen this work in past ages, and how it will be viewed now. In fact, such is the way it will always be viewed!"

I was stunned and speechless. I wasn't sure, and was afraid to use the word, fearing I might make a fool out of myself to this man I revered so much. But I took a chance. After a long silence between us I said, "Frater, are you suggesting, are you talking about the..." I was saving the potential humiliation of using the word that was on the tip of my tongue. Frater, seeing I was ill at ease over the matter, dropped the word from his lips as if it were a great weight. He spoke the word in a muffled whisper which betrayed a knowledgeable authority; as though even the mention of the word would engulf both of us in a darkly splendid, dual world of both nightmare and glory.

"Homunculus. Yes, Joe, that is what I am talking about. What I want you to do is to go back home and work as hard as you can on this year's work on antimony for Show and Tell next year. Do the extractions, make the Unfixed and Fixed Tinctures from the yellow, orange, and green glasses, bring samples of those raw glasses and the tinctures back with you next year to show the others, make the Kerkring Menstruum, and obtain the Oil of Antimony from the yellow and orange glass. You know how. Work on these things from now until April, when you are to begin collecting the electrified rainwater that Homer tells you about. You're going to run into problems because of air pollution, and will have to distill and re-electrify it. It's going to be a huge task, but you can do it over a couple of years. Say nothing to anyone about this. If you succeed in all of this, then you are to go on and 'generate' these animals as Homer gives, from the Gur. And make certain you have enough Gur from the putrefaction of the rainwater, because you will need it for the Homunculus."

I objected immediately that it was just too much work to do over the course of a year. But Frater insisted, and told me that if I kept at it, I could not only do the antimony work, but finish the Herbal Stones for demonstration in next year's Quinta Class as well.

(I had brought my four 'Stones-in-progress' to class, but only showed them to Frater because they were not fully mature. I was worried that if word got out I had brought them with me, I might be pushed to test them, and I knew they would not work at that point and I would only end up making a fool of myself in front of my classmates. To my surprise, Frater told me they were nearer to maturity than I thought. He instructed me on what to do when I returned to my own laboratory in order to bring them to term; this, so I could bring them back with me to next year's class for a final demonstration.) Therefore, along with the Herbal work, he insisted that I produce the tinctures of antimony, the Kerkring Menstruum, and the Oil of Antimony. Further, he insisted that by the end of next year, the re-electrified rain water would be putrefying on its own and would require no additional work from me until the following year.

In addition, he wanted me to write "...two perfectly clear scientific papers on the Homeric process..." which he would publish in the Society's Journal, *Essentia: Journal of Evolutionary Thought in Action*. He went on:

*"The first paper will be on the difficulties of collecting, distilling, and re-electrifying the rainwater. You will need **about 100 to 200 gallons**, if I remember correctly. The second paper will cover the actual generation of the animals themselves. If you succeed in getting the rainwater and doing what you must with it, it will not be difficult to further distill it into the Four Waters you will need to complete the work. Nor will it be difficult to generate the creatures. After you have finished all this, we will discuss the Homunculus together, privately. This is **our** goal. But first, **we** must do this Little Work of Water, so you can acquire the Keys to the Animal Kingdom of Nature. Then you will be able to **create** the Homunculus."*

I remember sitting still, staring at Frater across the lab bench, trying to absorb all he had just said. I also recall thinking how surreal our discussion had been, how my body felt stiff, and that all I could manage to think about was the utter impossibility of the workload over the next few years. I said nothing in reply. Then Frater looked me squarely in the eyes and said, "Do you accept the tasks?" I wanted to think it over first. But instead I heard myself say, "Yes."

He smiled very broadly, and gave a hearty laugh—one of the few times I ever heard him laugh. He was very excited, jumped up from his stool, clapped his hands, and as he left the lab in those early morning hours, he said,

"Oh yes. I discussed all of this with your friend, Israel Regardie. He'll be contacting you when you return home. He also has his assignments from me, but is very interested in this matter as well. The three of us will be working in tandem on these projects, so the two of you will be reporting your results directly to me. There is one more thing, Joe. Discuss this with no one, other than Regardie and myself. Understood?! I mean this. I am going to hold you to it."

I nodded agreement and told him I would not say a word to anyone. With that, he happily tapped the walls with his left hand as he walked to the door, disappeared into the darkness of the hallway, and returned to his home. Thus, the 'Trinity' as I still refer to it to this day, was formed.

I sat there until dawn, wondering what had happened, finally realizing what I had just gotten myself into. But there was no denying it. The entire concept of the Homunculus had always intrigued me. And if it meant that I had to go through all that Frater had outlined in order to enter into the darkest and most dangerous part of the world of alchemy, then so be it. I accepted my lot, and mentally began to prepare for the work that lay ahead.

I never believed in dragging my feet in anything, much less in occult matters. And since I was getting my mind in shape to deal with what was to come, I didn't wait to return home and have Regardie telephone me as Frater told me would happen. Instead, the next day during our class lunch break I walked to the corner restaurant and telephoned Regardie from a pay phone. As slowly and as accurately as I could I told him what happened between Frater and me the night before. At first, Regardie was beside himself. He told me,

"...you should have your head examined for agreeing to all that! When Albert told me during my class [he repeated Sexta that same year in May] what he intended to spring on you, I only laughed. Don't you see? It was all a setup! That's what Albert does! He got Nintzel to 'discover' that Homer manuscript and goad you with it, because he knew about your scientific work on this subject and that he could pull you into it! I knew all this from what he told me earlier this year, but I told him you'd never agree to it! There is just too much to do! It will take quite a few years of blindly-sustained effort; and with you holding a full-time job, and being married, I thought you would never agree to all that work! Now we're both in for it because I agreed I would accept the work if you did! Now I'm stuck! Thanks a lot! Call me when you get back home and we'll sort this mess out!"

It was clear that Frater had worked his way as usual, and that no matter how much Regardie complained, he too—as was his way—was not about to sit on his hands and do nothing. Even his failures in making the Herbal Stone amounted to nothing for him, because he was intent on succeeding in Alchemy no matter what. My agreement to Frater's demands—for really, that is what they were—my blunder in this matter, only served as a convenient excuse that allowed Regardie to accept Frater's work assignments without losing face over the issue. For it became very apparent to me throughout the years that although Regardie and Frater were friendly, they were no longer friends. The events of years ago; the arguments that resulted; the insults I found out each had leveled at one another during that 1958 meeting at Regardie's house when Frater insisted Regardie leave his California life and come with him to Salt Lake City; all had festered in the minds of both men, and had become irreconcilable. Neither could or would budge on these matters. And indeed, neither ever did.

When I returned home in early October of 1978, the first thing I did was to telephone Regardie and ask him what he had agreed to do for Frater. It was then that he elaborated on a fundamental problem in working in the Kingdom of Metals, which was a problem all of us in alchemy know all too well, that had to be scientifically addressed, and quickly, according to Frater. The problem is how to obtain the exact temperatures at which antimony trioxide will yield up the seven colors of its glass for making either the Fixed or Unfixed tinctures of this metal. According to alchemical lore, the importance of an antimony tincture obtained from the different colored glass of antimony lies in the powerful medicament properties of the tinctures. That is, the tinctures are used as medicaments that—according to the ancient alchemists—could be used by an individual to treat and cure a great spectrum of physical maladies and diseases: even that of cancer, as Basil Valentine explains in his classic work, *The Triumphal Chariot of Antimony*.

Thus, Frater assigned Regardie the task of determining those temperatures when using both the 'unfluxed' antimony trioxide, as well as the 'fluxed' trioxide (the process of fluxing involves addition of boron to the antimony trioxide—whether as a fume or sublimate, or as antimony trioxide produced by calcining antimony trisulfide to the trioxide state directly). To make such determinations however, requires a special furnace. Now, if a muffle furnace were used—at least, those that were available back in the late 1970s—a problem was immediately encountered. The electric muffle furnace such as the one I used to fuse my Herbal Stones would operate up to 1100–1200 degrees Celsius (2012–2192 degrees Fahrenheit), but it had two drawbacks. First, it had a small furnace cavity—usually a cube, 4 inches on a side—which allowed only small quantities of a

Israel Regardie & the Philosopher's Stone

substance to be heat-treated, coupled with the duty of holding these high temperatures for a fifteen-minute cycle. This means that the furnace had to be shut down after the cycle to allow the electric elements to cool down. This cool-down period usually took about ten hours, otherwise the electric elements would burn out. However, these electrically-driven units were equipped with a thermocouple and a temperature potentiometer which allows an accurate reading of the temperature of the cavity, and therefore of the substance being heated.

In the case of a gas muffle furnace, the gas used to drive the furnace, even in those days, was MAPP gas, produced by combining liquefied petroleum gas with methylacetylene-propadiene. This results in a highly stable, high energy fuel that offers excellent performance for heating, brazing, soldering, metallizing, flame cutting and flame-hardening. In short, this is a perfect gas for alchemical laboratory operations, including calcining, *etc*. And while the cavity of such a gas-powdered muffle furnace is much larger, and the high temperatures needed to turn the antimony trioxide into a glass could be maintained indefinitely, the temperature-sensing and read-out mechanism of such a furnace was/is very poor indeed. In short, you receive the colored glass you want with such a gas-powered furnace, but cannot necessarily reproduce the results the next time, owing to the erroneous temperature readings initially received. Unknown to me at the time, Frater had a plan to solve this problem.

At my 1977 Tertia Class, Frater approached me in the office one day, and said,

"You mentioned you were interested in designing and building an electric furnace that would solve all of our problems with antimony. I happened to mention this to Herbert K. [an older German living in Salt Lake who was a frequent visitor to the PRS], and he said he could out do you any day on making such a furnace. What should I tell him?"

I was very young then, flew off the handle, and told Frater,

"You tell K. for me to have his furnace here for class next year, and I'll have mine shipped to PRS in advance. We'll set both of them up side-by-side, and we'll see who out does who!"

Frater smiled and said he would tell him. I did exactly that. I designed and built a special electric furnace that used ordinary house current that reached **1800 degrees Celsius (3272 degrees Fahrenheit) and which operated for hours at a time**. The furnace was made of heavy gauge sheet metal standing 24 inches high, and 10 inches on each side. It was rectangular in shape, had a core that consisted of a cylindrical, pure, fused aluminum oxide crucible 8 inches in height and 6 inches in diameter. This crucible was situated in the furnace cavity by surrounding it with diatomaceous earth—a natural, very efficient insulator. A removable top, made of an 8-inch square of *Cast-Set* pourable refractory material, was provided for accessing the crucible within the furnace cavity. The crucible itself consisted of 12 windings of 0.032 inches diameter, Cromel-Alumel, a high temperature-yielding electric furnace wire. When connected to a variable transformer (Variac) and the voltage adjusted, all one had to do was to note the voltage being used that produced a given colored glass of antimony. To accurately determine the temperature of the furnace core, I provided—as part of the furnace setup—an optical pyrometer as well. This is an instrument that measures radiation—in this case, the glow of the furnace cavity—and converts it into an electrical current in the pyrometer, and registers the corresponding temperature on a special meter.

Thus, by noting the voltage of the Variac and the temperature read-out of the optical pyrometer, the laboratory worker can, not only pour a given color glass of antimony, but repeat the process time after time, with all the guesswork and lack of experimental reproducibility eliminated. The complete unit was shipped to Frater at the PRS in time for my 1978 Quarta Class. When class began, I

Israel Regardie & the Philosopher's Stone 127

demonstrated the furnace in front of Frater and my fellow classmates. It worked flawlessly. In one afternoon, I was able to pour all of the seven colors of the glass of antimony, and was able to reproduce the voltages and temperatures at will. I did this alone, however, as Herbert K. never showed up that year, and neither did his furnace. The complete furnace was donated to Frater for use in the laboratories, so that our alchemical work could now proceed on a consistent, massive scale.

What I did not know until the conversation I had with Regardie when I returned home from that class, was that the furnace I designed, built and donated to the PRS, was now being loaned to Regardie so he could make the experimental determinations of heating times, voltages, and temperatures needed to both make the different colored glasses of antimony, and to reproduce the processes at will! As Regardie told me during that conversation,

"Albert decided that there was no one he trusted sufficiently at the school to do the work. Everyone who came, went. And those who said they wanted to help always found reason to conveniently disappear when the time for work had come. That's why he asked me to do the job. He knew I didn't have the technical background to do it but didn't care, since he insisted a guy could learn all the lab stuff on his own, anyway. What he did like is that I stick to what I start until I either succeed or fail. And in his own words, he said, 'That's all anyone can ask of a man!' So now I have to do my job too!"

Thus, now Regardie had no excuse for not being able to do as Frater wanted. Frater had cut him off at every turn, in one way or another. To keep his part of the bargain so to speak, Regardie had to rent a small U-Haul truck, drive from Los Angeles to Salt Lake City, pick up the furnace assembly along with a few hundred pounds of antimony trioxide (fume) and antimony trisulfide, return to Los Angeles, and get to work! I can't tell the reader how 'pleased' he was with me over these new developments! (Further details of Regardie's work with the furnace and the determination of the times and temperatures needed to produce the different colored glasses of antimony will follow in Chapter Six.)

Regardie asked me the specifics of my own assignments. To my surprise, he was not as interested in the further work with antimony I was now obliged to carry out, nor with getting my Herbal Stones to mature. What he was most interested in was the Homeric work in all of its phases, especially the possibility of creating a Homunculus. It was then that he confided in me on a matter that had concerned him for some time; a matter that was a dark corner in Magic, and which to the best of his knowledge had never been attempted previously, at least, not correctly, as he insisted. And that was a ritual technique for the creation of a 'Magical Child.' Not the New Age nonsense type, mixed with various levels of Tantra, psychological taboos, and drunken, free-for-all sex mixed with enough mumbo-jumbo to "...gag a maggot..." as Regardie put it, but the "...real thing..." to coin his phrase. That is, this ritual process ends in the actual creation of a physical body that would house this 'Child.' One "...the world would never forget," as Regardie said.

This manuscript gave a process by which a man and woman—using the normal method of biological procreation—would conceive a fetus that would immediately be inhabited by an advanced soul personality. A soul that had reincarnated many times, and one adept in the magical arts and sciences. This child, when mature, would become aware of its own advanced nature and be able to pick up where it left off as it were, and once again resume its magical work in the world, and do so at a very early age. Regardie also reminded me that at one time he had shown me the manuscript in question: the privately printed document that gave the full rite for the creation of this Magical Child. He went on to say that when he had shown it to me, he had considered me too young to be in possession of it, even though I was twenty-four years old at the time and married. But now things had changed. As he phrased it,

"I think the time has come when you and your wife should consider initiating this process. I can't think of anyone better suited for the task, because both of you could give the Child what he or she needs as it grows to adulthood. It's something to consider."

At that point, I told him we did not intend to have any children due to my scientific work and the commitment I had made to that work years ago. He understood, but insisted I have a copy of the manuscript, and sent it to me a few weeks later. That manuscript is still in my possession. While my wife, Darlene, and I never used it, I consider it to be one of the strangest documents ever to fall into my hands. It contains ritual instruction the likes of which I have never seen, before or since—be it of the New Age type or Old System Magic variety. In some oblique way it has a slight—very slight— resemblance to an all but forgotten Old System Magic ritual. But even here, the Old System Magic rite bears only the most indirect and cursory resemblance to that process outlined in the manuscript Regardie gave to me. Still, Regardie believed that the creation of a Magical Child should be attempted. Nevertheless, after my courteous refusal during this one episode regarding the matter, Regardie and I never discussed it again. Instead, we turned our attention toward the work Frater had set out for us.

Regardie and I spent two weeks going over the *Golden Chain* together, his pointing out this, and asking that, with my doing the same to him. Even though Frater had instructed both of us to report our results directly to him, we felt certain he would have no objections to our sharing our results with each other. And indeed, he did not. In fact, when I asked him about this a few weeks later, he said, "Oh, absolutely! You and Israel have to work closely on these things, because two heads are always better than one!" And so, we did. In the course of things, Regardie either revealed something to me that I feel he may have regretted, or else told it purposely but in such a way as to get me thinking. If it was intentional, I still don't know his motive for doing so to this day. He told me,

"You probably picked up Albert's familiarity about the Homer process when he first sprung it on you, but in case you didn't, I feel it is only fair to tell you that he did these experiments himself long ago—on the Water Work I mean, and on the generation of those small animals as Homer calls them. And he succeeded in it too, very well from what I saw of it. But he could not go on with the attempt to create a Homunculus because of his damn moral belief nonsense, and so that's why he needs you. He wants you to take it as far as you can, so he can find out what he felt forbidden to do because of that moralistic nonsense of his!"

It all fit. When Frater had that conversation in the laboratory with me that night, it was quite obvious he was more than academically interested. Otherwise, how would he have known how many gallons of electrified rainwater I need to collect to start the process? Or else what was the basis of his remark that night, "*...about 100–200 gallons* you'll need, *if I remember correctly.*" I wondered about this and about his moral convictions in stopping short of experimenting with the Homunculus, to be sure. But then, I felt I understood Frater's deep sense of Christian morality, and actually admired him for it. Under no circumstances did I see his goading me into doing what he could not—would not—do as being hypocritical. I thought it was quite intelligent of him to make use of me in this way, especially since my own moral convictions at the time were anything but well defined. The truth of the matter is that I would have done whatever was necessary to succeed in creating the Homunculus, and as the reader will see in later chapters, I did.

While I set to work immediately on doing exactly what Frater had instructed, and in the way he instructed me to do it, Regardie busied himself by driving to PRS, getting the furnace, the antimony trioxide and trisulfide and the other laboratory paraphernalia he needed to begin his temperature, time, and voltage measurement. From October 1978 through April 1979 I worked as hard as I could. And by that April, I had not only obtained the Unfixed and Fixed Tinctures of Antimony from the yellow, orange, and green Glass of Antimony—and these, directly from antimony trioxide after calcining pounds of antimony trisulfide from which I then made the glasses of antimony—but additionally, I had experimentally determined the temperatures required to turn the trioxide into these three colors of glass.

Since the quantities of the glasses of antimony I had to make for my own purposes were much smaller than the quantities Regardie had to produce, I was able to find the melting points for three of the colors—orange, yellow, and green—quite easily by using my electric muffle furnace, repeating the process until I was satisfied, and then 'fed' these temperatures to Regardie. But since the four other colors required temperatures my electric muffle furnace could not reach, Regardie was on his own in determining them. Nevertheless, the few temperatures I found helped him "...get my feet wet in this work..." as he put it, and so my efforts were at least of some help. (The reader should remember that each color requires not only a different temperature, but a different time exposure to the temperature(s) as well, to assure that the cooled Glass of Antimony results in the color desired: red, orange, yellow, violet, green, blue, or black. There are always problems with exact temperature determinations for this work as previously discussed, not to mention other antimony preparation techniques, such as the addition of a 'fluxing agent' to the antimony trioxide. This procedure of fluxing complicated accurate temperature-determination measurements all the more, as the reader will soon learn of further in the next chapter.)

Additionally, by April of 1979, I had succeeded in producing large quantities of the Kerkring Menstruum, respectable quantities of the Oil of Antimony, and had finished the operations that finally took my four Herbal Stones to maturity. Finally, in April of that year, since I had all of these preliminary results set aside for the upcoming October Quinta Class, I turned my attention to the Water Work proper.

But two questions remained unanswered for both Regardie and me. First: We knew Frater already had approximate temperatures and exposure times for producing the seven different colored glasses of antimony. He not only told us this in class, but had shown us the different colored glasses. So why did he require the more extensive determinations to which he had set Regardie to do? Second: He had many gas-powered furnaces available at the PRS, and did have some thermocouples capable of giving fairly accurate readings of those temperatures. This being so, why did he require me to design and build an electric furnace capable of sustained activity at very high temperatures, and one capable of giving extremely accurate temperature measurements?

Regardie and I wondered about these things and discussed them at length. Lacking further data however, the best we could come up with was pure conjecture, which availed us nothing, and only served to irritate us. Regardie especially felt this way due to his history with Frater. His final comment on these matters before we ceased our curiosity and returned to our respective work was,

"Joe, you and I both know that Albert is using me in some way. Your being used is clear enough: that damned Christian morality of his has you doing things he forbids himself to do. But why me? I feel like a rat in a trap, running some damn maze of Albert's design. But I guess we'll never know."

Regardie's speculation about not knowing why Frater had him do the work with antimony was short-lived. For in December of 1978 Regardie's patience was at an end, and another showdown between those two was about to occur. But it would not end there, for yet another would follow in the Spring of 1979.

Chapter Six

Israel Regardie & the Mineral Kingdom of Nature

Throughout the Fall and Winter of 1978, while I was busy with my alchemical assignments, Regardie was busy doing his—or so I thought. But only later would I would find out he had problems from the outset. The extensive set of instructions I had written up for Frater on how to use the furnace and pyrometer correctly, as well as the electrical schematics and blueprints that explained their inner functioning in detail, had disappeared. And for some reason, Regardie was reluctant to discuss the matter with either Frater or myself. At least, that's how it appeared to me when the issue first surfaced.

It was not until early December of 1978 during a telephone conversation I had with Frater that I found out that there were problems. After telling Frater of the progress I had made thus far, he sighed deeply and asked if I had spoken to Israel lately. I told him since it is our custom to telephone each other at least three times a week, that yes, I had spoken to him only two days earlier. Then Frater asked me, "Did he mention anything to you about the problems he's having with the furnace and pyrometer?" My heart jumped into my throat, fearing the worst: that something had happened to either the furnace or its temperature measuring instrument, and that I would somehow have to find the time and money to build and ship another one to him. I told Frater this was the first I heard of it, and asked what the problem was.

I remember vividly how relieved I was when Frater told me, "...I received a letter—not a telephone call, mind you—but a letter from Israel telling me that something must have happened to the instructions as he could not find them, and so had not been doing any work these past two months!" I didn't know what else to say to Frater and so I simply replied, "At least that's all the trouble! Thank heavens for that! I'll call him, find out what happened, and see where we stand." I called several times that night, but Regardie was unavailable.

Finally, two days later I reached him, and told him of my conversation with Frater. I asked him if the instructions, schematics, and blueprints were indeed missing and if they were, why didn't he ask me to draw up another set of instructions for him, and whether he was going to do the work he had agreed to. It seemed to me that Regardie—always forthright and direct about everything—may have had a rethink on the matter, and had either backed out on the agreement, or was considering backing out.

At first there was a deafening silence. Then suddenly he exploded into so many emotional pieces. After a torrent of curses leveled at Frater, he began to cough and snort like a person gasping for air. He asked angrily,

"Do you hear that, Joe? Do you know how I got this lung condition in the first place? By working with that damn antimony trisulfide years ago before I knew what I was doing, that's how! The arsenic and sulfur got into the deep part of the lungs and everything down there is clogged up! That's why I have to take my time these days when I walk or am physically active! I have Albert to thank for all of this because he didn't know what the hell he was doing with all that stuff back then, yet he was teaching it to fools like me who went off half-cocked and started working with it! That's how this came about! And now you call me and tell me that Albert tells you about

some missing instructions and you insinuate I'm sitting on my rump, not doing my job? Well, let me tell you something, and listen goddamn well! I don't need you or Albert! I don't need anyone at all!"

I tried to explain I was only trying to find out what the problem was, or indeed if there was a problem, and that is why I called. I was not trying to upset him by any means! But Regardie was on a tirade, the obvious product of his years of anger toward Frater, the difficulties he encountered when working with the Herbal Stone, and his earlier experiments with antimony and the harmful effects they had upon his health. Fearful, I kept quiet and let him go on until he exhausted his wrath because it had to come out. After some time, Regardie calmed down and began to speak quietly. His first words were ones of reconciliation through an apology. For it was his opinion that both of us had been duped by Frater once again, and for what reason neither of us could ever figure out. He continued.

"I telephoned Albert weeks ago and we had it out—again! I did not send him a letter as he told you. I told him that the instructions for the furnace and that optical thing were missing from the boxes he had crated up, waiting for me when I drove to the Society to pick them up. I told him how fed up I was with him and his people's incompetence, and was near my breaking point with all of it! He said he understood, apologized for the miscommunication, and suggested I get a hold of you and have you make another set for me. Albert said they were using your original blueprints and write-ups on the furnace at Paralab [more about this commercial alchemical or 'spagyric' venture of Frater's will be explained later] to see if we can have more of Joe's furnaces built. He thought there shouldn't be a problem with the blueprints and instructions he had provided.

"When I asked him why he needed more of them built, all he said was that they were for a new project for Paralab. I asked him if he would at least make me a copy of your instructions because of all the diagrams and electrical blueprints that were in it. He said that

he would but never did. So here I sit. I was going to call and ask you to redo all of them for me [blueprint reproduction machines were nowhere available either in or near the small town where I was living in 1978] figuring he would put me off, but I didn't. And I didn't, because I knew that you were under a very heavy workload as it is.

"So now you know. Here's Albert again, giving you assignments, giving me assignments, and then sabotaging them for some new pie-in-the-sky idea of his! I'm not going to let this go! If you can't redo those plans for me, then Albert will just have to send me your originals whether he likes it or not! Otherwise, he can take this assignment he gave me and..."

Now, Regardie did not have true emphysema at that point, or so he insisted to me. Rather, as he explained to me in detail, his lungs were burned or congested as he preferred to call it, due to arsenic and sulfur poisoning from his experiments, and which had landed him in a hospital for several days. But in fact, antimony trioxide is only weakly absorbed by the digestive system, the main route of exposure being by inhalation of the dust, with its elimination from the body being slow. This retarded elimination however, leads to a risk of chronic toxicity in the form of pneumoconiosis if there are continued exposures through inhalation.

Acute poisoning is very rare indeed, the signs of such poisoning pointing to anything but poisoning. Namely, the symptoms that most frequently occur are vomiting, abdominal pain, irritation of the mucous membranes and diarrhea. All of these problems are normally associated with a digestive tract disorder, and it is not uncommon for cardiac irregularities to occur, as I found out myself during my early days of experimenting with this metal. Since the symptoms that occur are more often associated with the ingestion of other more water-soluble compounds, difficulties in diagnosis are certain to occur. Add to this Regardie's refusal to tell his physician what he was doing when he had his first accident with the antimony, and one can understand how the treatments that existed for this type of poisoning at the time were never applied to him.

Regardie told me he did his research on the matter and found that chronic poisoning by antimony trioxide was rare, with the main symptoms being irritation of the respiratory tract and skin, along with the characteristic pneumoconiosis which is visible on chest X-rays. And indeed, as he explained to me, the condition did show up on his X-rays, as did a severe irritation of his upper respiratory tract, along with brownish patches on his skin. All this after his first accident with the metal. And there it was. Regardie was displaying the symptoms of a continuing chronic state of poisoning that could eventually have a deleterious effect on his health, if accidental exposure to the fumes of antimony trisulfide continued to occur.

Thus, Regardie was genuinely and justifiably fearful of further work with antimony trioxide and let me know it in no uncertain terms. He also made Frater aware of it for "…the umteenth time…" when he kept his promise and telephoned him immediately after our telephone conversation of that night. To Regardie's surprise however, Frater began the conversation by telling Regardie that the original instructions, schematics, and blueprints for the furnace had been duplicated completely, and a set was now on the way to him! Frater also explained that their attempts to have the furnace duplicated in Salt Lake City failed miserably. The quotes given them by several companies were simply too high, and to have twelve such furnaces reproduced was way beyond their budget.

When Regardie enquired as to why they needed so many units, Frater finally explained that it was his intention to use the furnaces to produce both the Unfixed and Fixed Tinctures of Antimony of the seven colors of glass that correspond to the Seven Planetary Rays, such that the tinctures could be sold commercially through the Paracelsus Laboratories under their "Natural Herbal and Mineral Preparations with a Difference" marketing program. He was very disappointed that they were not able to do this, but held onto his dream by telling Regardie,

"*Yes, it is a shame, but only for now. If we obtain additional funding—and I think this likely—then we will have the additional furnaces built and be able to market the tinctures. If by chance additional funding falls through, there still might be a possibility that we can produce the tinctures on a limited basis, and use the proceeds from those sales to eventually have the other furnaces built. I see no reason why this cannot work, so those are my thoughts on the matter at this point.*"

Regardie saw this as "…another exercise in Albert's delusions. But who knows? He is so damned insistent he may just pull it off!" When Regardie received the furnace papers in the mail a few days later, he placed his own health risk concerns aside once more, and set to work immediately in the small shed in his backyard. Using the data I sent him regarding the temperatures needed to produce the first three colors of glass: orange, yellow and green, he reproduced them easily during December of 1978 and verified that the temperatures were indeed correct. The remaining four colors of the glass of antimony—red, violet, blue and black—had yet to be determined by him: a project he reserved for January of 1979 onward.

Regardie was now used to working with the furnace and the optical pyrometer, and was fascinated with their working. For in truth, while Regardie maintained that he had no mechanical ability or dexterity whatsoever, his intellect was so superior that he could adopt or mimic whatever physical skill he needed at any given time. It was only his chosen reluctance to put his hand to a physical or mundane task that prevented him from accomplishing more than he did in the physical realm of things. Indeed, his magical weapons alone—which I personally handled in April 1986 while at the Israel Regardie Foundation, Golden Dawn Temple and Society in Sedona,

Arizona—were stunning testaments to the powerful and effective mechanical ability that he did possess when he chose to possess it.

The idea that Frater Albertus conceived of—for example, producing both the Fixed and Unfixed Tinctures of Antimony, and those from the seven different glasses of this oxide—offers a fitting place for a discussion of Paralab, an offshoot of the Paracelsus Laboratories. For it was against this backdrop that Regardie labored in his attempts to accurately determine the temperatures of the various colored glass, coupled with Frater's desire to make such unheard-of medicaments available to the public at large through this strange business venture.

What then was this Paralab enterprise, and how did it not only impact Regardie's situation, but all of us who were privileged to work with Frater Albertus in one way or another? For make no mistake about it. Frater's sole attempt was to bring Alchemy "Out into the open; into the light of science" as he continually preached. And to do this, he determined that "…only when everyday people are uplifted by having their physical ailments cured, will those in present day power come to realize the importance of this art and science, and extend to us the resources we need to make this plane [of existence] a healthier, better, and happier place to live…" as he explained to us during one of our classes.

He was convinced of this, and so used the Paracelsus Research Society for two purposes. First, to school us in practical laboratory alchemy so we could continue on after his departure. And second, as a parent organization for the offshoot he had planned, of which Paralab was only the first. Thus, Paralab was formed.

As Frater Albertus' contributions to Alchemy are every bit as important, historically, as those of Paracelsus, I feel his legacy as to the purpose of Paralab and its parent, Paracelsus Laboratories, should be cited in his own words, using his own public marketing literature. As I saved all of the materials from my PRS years, I will now cite from one of those pieces of sales literature below:

❄❄❄❄

Paracelsus Laboratories
Natural Herbal and Mineral Preparations with a Difference
Paralab—A Corporation Combining Old and Proven Knowledge with Current Technology

Paralab was established in 1972 in the beautiful Salt Lake Valley at the base of the Wasatch Mountains. At this location the exclusive Paralab products are manufactured.

These products are unique because they are pure, potent derivatives of natural botanical, mineral and metallic essentials produced by our exclusive method, which retains the three essentials: spirit, ethereal oils, and mineral salts.

These products are prepared by the skill and precision of a specially trained staff, who, like the craftsmen of old, take great care and pride in their work. Paralab's main concern is to manufacture preparations of high quality. We select those products which come from nature, rather than chemically synthesized substitutes.

Each member of our staff is enthusiastic to be part of Paralab! We are committed to serving you, our customer most efficiently, and through our sales program, making these products available on a wide scale to all those who would benefit thereby.

Paralab products are shipped to customers worldwide, and our office is kept busy by this growing demand.

The Preparation of Paralab Products is the Reason for Their Great Effectiveness

"Spagyric" is a Greek word consisting of "Spao," to separate, and "Ageiro," to combine. Paralab's spagyric products are obtained by taking a substance, such as a plant, and separating it into its three essential parts, known as the essential oil, spirit (obtained by natural fermentation), and its minerals in the form of salts. These must be separated without adding anything foreign to them, such as acids or alkalies. After separation, these three essentials are then purified to remove all extraneous substances. Once completely purified they are recombined into potent non-toxic preparations.

At Last Here Are Products Which Retain The Total Virtues Of Their Herbal & Mineral Contents In An Effective & Easy To Take Form

List of Products:

Tincture Paracelsus: This is one of many similar formulas used by Paracelsus, which he proposed was good for the entire circulatory system, fatigue, and symptoms of early aging. It contains over twenty different herbs including: [here was an extensive list of the herbs used].

Tincture Albertus: We all know how valuable iron is for the blood and the maintenance of a healthy body, full of energy and vitality. Paralab uses only the native iron for our Tincture Albertus. Plants and herbal products with their inherent vitamins and minerals retain their essence or life when they are not subjected to high degrees of heat, and so also, do the minerals and metals retain their life-force if they are handled properly and not subjected to a smelting process. [List of contents then follows.]

Tincture Hermes: Another one of Paracelsus' formulas which is similar to what he observed was good for soothing the nervous system. It was to be especially useful when nerves were overtaxed. No claim is made that this is undisputed evidence. It contains no narcotics or barbiturates. [List of contents follows.]

Tincture St. Germain: Comte de St. Germain supposedly originated this tincture for aiding digestion and the relief of flatulence. [List of contents was here.]

Swedish Tincture: The formula for this herbal tincture was discovered among the belongings of a Swedish medical doctor after he died at the ripe old age of 104 when he fell to his death while horseback riding. He was reported as using this formula for expelling poisons from the body, relieving pain, combating fever, and cleansing sugar from the blood. With this herbal tincture he claimed to have helped his grandfather live to be 130 years of age, his father live to 113, and his mother to attain 107 years. [Contents of this tincture are then listed.]

Para Hair Herbal: This is a spagyric product containing only natural ingredients, used to add luster to dull, lifeless hair. [List of contents.]

Para Skin Rub: For external use in aches, pains and discomforts, with superior penetrative virtues. Especially beneficial when taken with Tincture Albertus or Swedish Tincture. [List of contents.]

Venus De Milo Skin Lotion: A most unusual delicately scented vanishing cream-lotion invigorating the skin with a blend of

Israel Regardie & the Philosopher's Stone   143

fresh fruits and all natural ingredients, which are known for stimulating and toning the skin. [List of contents.]

Aurora Beauty Cream: A superb nourishing and moisturizing cream especially prepared for use on delicate tissues of the face, eyes, and other areas of the body. Excellent as a night cream or for use under make-up. Available in rose or bergamot scent. [List of contents.]

Oil of Egg: Oil of egg is found prescribed and used by the great physician, Paracelsus. His prescriptions requiring oil of egg were compounded for external use involving healing of tissues due to wounds, abrasions, etc.

Eucalyptus Oil: This rare Blue Mallee oil shipped from Australia is superior to other species of eucalyptus and is known for its excellence in both internal and external use. It is a powerful antiseptic and is used extensively in conditions such as influenza, bronchitis, sore throat, congestion, etc. It is often rubbed on rheumatic joints, or on the chest and back for colds and asthma.

Paralab Mineral Salt Solutions: These are not to be confused with the conventional tablet form of tissue remedies. These mineral salts in solution are more easily assimilated, as they do not have to go through the digestive process. For further information contact Paralab today!

Paralab Herbal Extracts: Man has known for centuries the importance of herbs. Many of our parents and especially grandparents used herbs to assist them in their everyday life. Today, you can find many forms of these herbs for sale, but as far as we at Paralab are aware, none of these have all three essentials, spagyrically separated and prepared, as the Paralab Herbal Extracts do. Following are a few of the herbal tinctures available through Paralab, although others may be prepared upon request: Chamomile, Chickweed, Comfrey, Dandelion

Root, Fennel, Gentian, Hawthorne, Juniper, Melissa, Mountain Sage, Mullein, Valerian, Watercress, and Yarrow.

Paralab Natural Mineral Water: Hydrotherapy is the oldest healing method known to man. To heal the body with water is also the simplest, most effective way. The unique difference in Paralab's Natural Mineral Water is that it has been separated into its three essential constituents, namely, alkaline, acid, and neutralized properties by electro-dialysis, without adding anything foreign. Available throughout the United States. This water is also lightly carbonated for use as an excellent table water. Presently available only in Utah.

Why import from foreign markets products available in your own country? This underground water supply comes from deep strata. The water has come into contact with the Minerals we find at that depth. Whatever Minerals dissolve in the water, will be contained in the water as it rises to the surface. This Artesian Well water has been tested by the Salt Lake County and Utah State Department of Health and found to be free from harmful bacteria.

Paralab Elixir of Spring: Contains pure iron derived from nature's own iron obtained in a special process. Reliable and pure plant extracts including Hawthorne, known for ages as an excellent herb to strengthen the heart, fortify this tonic. Added to this is the mineral salt in solution of your own zodiacal sun sign to give the balance needed for a healthy body free from toxins. [List of contents.]

Aries — Mar. 21 - Apr. 20 — Potassium Phosphate
Taurus — Apr. 21 - May 20 — Sodium Sulphate
Gemini — May 21 - June 20 — Potassium Chloride
Cancer — June 21 - July 20 — Calcium Fluoride
Leo — July 21 - Aug. 20 — Magnesium Phosphate
Virgo — Aug. 21 - Sept. 20 — Potassium Sulphate
Libra — Sept. 21 - Oct. 20 — Sodium Phosphate
Scorpio — Oct. 21 - Nov. 20 — Calcium Sulphate

Israel Regardie & the Philosopher's Stone 145

Sagittarius — Nov. 21 – Dec. 20 — Silica
Capricorn — Dec. 21 – Jan. 20 — Calcium Phosphate
Aquarius — Jan. 21 – Feb. 20 — Sodium Chloride
Pisces — Feb. 21 – Mar. 20 — Iron Phosphate

(The back of the brochure is filled with customer testimonials from people around the world. Interestingly, on page 2 is a testimonial to Mr. Albert Riedel written by Dr. I.F. Regardie.)

❊❊❊❊

In January of 1979, Regardie and I had several long conversations prior to him beginning his work with the furnace and optical pyrometer to find the temperatures at which the blue, red, violet, and black transparent glasses of antimony could be produced. Having known of his burned lung condition as I preferred to call it, and it having been due to his earlier work with the antimony, I cautioned him about calcining the antimony trisulfide in close quarters. I was in that small shed of his in his backyard, and had a strong mental image of it fixed in my mind. I asked him to set up two fans across from each other, one in the window in the west and one in the doorway in the east so he would have plenty of ventilation. I also pleaded with him to enter the shed only every so often just to stir the antimony and to check on its progress.

He only laughed and told me I was a young pup compared to him, that he had the experience of having his lungs damaged from this work and not me, and that he knew what to do. Then we discussed the furnace and his upcoming search for the remaining four colors of the Glass of Antimony and that—as he found out from his work with the furnace the month before—there was no reason for him to worry about the fumes generated by melting the antimony trioxide into a glass. That is, provided he kept the window and door fan going while he processed the glass! After these conversations, I went back to my own alchemical work, and Regardie set about his.

The weeks passed. The early Spring of 1979 was upon us. As Regardie's glass pouring attempts continued, it became clear to both of us he had run into more problems. Try as he may—with both the fluxed and unfluxed antimony trioxide—he could not produce the remaining four colors of the Glass of Antimony. He had successfully recorded all of the temperatures obtained with the optical pyrometer, as well as the voltages from the Variac's voltmeter. He had calcined pounds of the trisulfide into trioxide, and had produced batches of the trioxide both with the boron-fluxing agent and without it, and had developed a perfect technique for working with the furnace. Indeed, he was even astute in extracting the furnace core from the furnace, removing the high-temperature coil from the pure, fused, Aluminum Oxide crucible, rewinding it with new Cromel-Alumel I had provided for him, replacing the core, and even rewiring it!

In short, Regardie had done everything correctly! Yet when he reached temperatures above 1400 degrees Centigrade—temperatures at which the red, blue, violet and black glasses of antimony are produced—he would either receive a 'slag' which is a product that resembles a waste product usually derived from melting mineral ores, or else he would obtain a brownish translucent—not transparent—material!

When we discussed this and I brought up the possibility of his under-developed Interior Realm—meaning, of course, his possible under-developed mystical aspects of consciousness as opposed to his developed magical talents—as being the root causes of both his failure to produce an Herbal Stone and now the inability to pour the remaining four colors of the Glass of Antimony, he immediately dismissed this possibility, reverting to his belief that a certain type of physical thinking was necessary for one to succeed in the deeper realms of alchemy.

I told him I disagreed with this completely and reminded him that I had seen—as he had as well—people succeed in a given alchemical operation, while a given student standing next to them failed, even though all had used the same materials, lab equipment, *etc.* But Regardie dismissed this. He held firm to his belief in the idea that a certain type of physical thought was necessary when working with the more complex areas of alchemy, and would hear no more of it. And while he and I had grown quite close throughout the years, there was only so far I would go. I was, quite frankly, very fearful of incurring his wrath, for Regardie was capable of great rage and anger, as I had previously found out for myself.

Seeing that Regardie disagreed with my 'Inner Realm' concept and I with his 'physical thinking' model, our subsequent telephone conversations focused on finding one or more possible mundane explanations as to why he had and was still experiencing problems in his alchemical endeavors. During one discussion in the middle of March of 1979, he suddenly did an about face and agreed that perhaps his Interior Realm state—or his "Mystical Development" as he now termed it—was the real reason for his failures in anything beyond the more elementary work in alchemy.

I remember how sad he sounded when he said,

"What if this is true, Joe? What recourse do I have then? I never found any mystical path satisfying, Albert's least of all. So, what do I do now?"

I didn't know what else to say except to remind him he was the one who had taught me Magic, and that he refers to me as the young one so that I didn't know what to say. Regardie laughed and dismissed the matter saying,

"To hell with it all! There's got to be some other reason for my lab failures. I'll find the answer myself and I'd better do it damn fast. I don't want to lose any more time! I have a lot of alchemy to do—especially the work on lead—and so had better get myself straight if I'm to do it!" And so, Francis Israel Regardie went back to his

furnace, pyrometer, and antimony, in that tiny shed in his backyard, grimly determined to find the answer.

I did not call him again until the following week—the last week of March 1979 as my notes from that time show, due to my work load, both alchemical and personal. As was my custom, I would always call Regardie on Monday and Wednesday, with him usually calling me on Friday. If there was something special or pressing on the agenda, one of us would also call the other on a Thursday as well. Saturday was out, except for emergency calls. And since he never answered his telephone on Sunday, that day was completely restricted, being his sacred time for winding down. I failed to reach him on Monday. Wednesday came and went, but there was no call from him. Finally, on Thursday I called numerous times throughout the day and night, but again without result. I was going to continue telephoning the following day, Friday, starting very early in the morning, when Regardie telephoned me at seven a.m. my time, something he had never done before. Then he explained what happened.

After our last conversation, Regardie determined to succeed in obtaining the temperatures of the four remaining colors of the Glass of Antimony, no matter what. So, on that Saturday he secreted himself away in his house and shed, turned his telephone off, and went to work around the clock. As he was working, an idea came to him. He explained:

"What if the temperatures above 1400 degrees Centigrade produce the clear, transparent Glass of Antimony, and not from the calcined trioxide, whether fluxed or unfluxed, but from the raw ore itself? That is, directly from the antimony trisulfide as it is mined from the earth? What if these higher temperatures produce some type of chemical reaction that somehow gives the colors, red, violet, black, and blue?

Israel Regardie & the Philosopher's Stone

"After all, all of us had seen and handled the seven colors of the Glass of Antimony ourselves at some point in our PRS career. But no one knew the exact temperatures or procedures needed to produce these other colors of the glass. Even Frater Albertus alluded that the temperatures and conditions necessary to pour these other colors are not well known, and had to be explored further. And wasn't this the reason he had you design and build the furnace and donate the pyrometer? Wasn't this also the reason he had me try to experimentally determine the temperatures using the furnace and optical device?"

These were the thoughts that ran through Regardie's mind at the time. But on Sunday night, very late, something happened; his worst fears had come to pass. Whether due to exhaustion, fear of not succeeding, that intensity that affects all who are so wrapped up in their work they begin to have lapses of awareness, or a combination of these and other factors, Regardie made an error. After placing a large quantity of the raw antimony trisulfide ore in the furnace core and running the furnace temperature up to 1555 degrees Centigrade, he lost track of the time and removed the 8-inch square top after "...only a few minutes heating instead of the full ten minutes I thought it should take." The result was that Regardie received a full blast of the superheated sulfur-arsenic steam that was being driven off the antimony.

When the cloud of gas hit him in the face, it not only singed his face, it triggered his natural reaction to draw breath; as one does when suddenly taken aback by something. And breathe he did. Deeply. The poisonous compounds entered his already damaged lungs, and he began to choke. After making his way back to his house, he called for an ambulance and was taken to a local hospital where he spent the better part of the week. When anyone would ask him why he was in the hospital—his clients especially queried him as he told me, since all of his appointments were cancelled during that hospital stay—Regardie was so private in this matter of his alchemical pursuits that he told them and most others that he was in for a prostate operation. This, as he related to me months later, I also suspected that he was embarrassed at his apparent carelessness in carrying out the production of the glass. For when he told me of this prostate dodge, he related it with great venom in his voice; as a hate that could not be contained any longer, and just had to spill over:

"It's none of anyone's business why I was in there, Joe, and they got what they deserve! I'm tired of people sticking their noses into my private business! It's been going on for over forty years, and I've had it with all of them, their 'interest' and 'concern' for my 'welfare,' all of it! I'm so tired of everything and of people, and their goddamn shenanigans!"

It didn't take long for him to contact Frater Albertus either. After that Friday telephone call from Regardie, he telephoned Frater the next day and the two had what was—in Regardie's opinion—their "...worst argument ever..." As he later told me, he "...laid the dead dog where it belonged: on Albert's doorstep! I told him straight this was all his doing, this nonsense of trying to find temperatures that he couldn't or wouldn't try to find himself, and I told him what he could do with the assignment he gave me! I told him I was done with it, finished, fed up, and he could take this furnace and optical thing back and do with it what he wanted, because I had enough!" Thus, Regardie backed out of attempting to find the exact temperatures which would produce the seven colors of the Glass of Antimony, which would have allowed their tinctures to be manufactured on an industrial-type scale.

It was now abundantly clear that Regardie was through with anymore hardcore alchemical experimentation, at least as far as producing the seven colors of the Glass of Antimony was concerned. And certainly, no one can fault him for that. He did everything he could to advance the art and science that alchemy is, as well as to advance himself along the way. But as had come to be the case, his interior problems overcame his best efforts, as he finally and freely admitted to later on.

That Sunday evening, the day after Regardie's and Frater Albertus' "worst argument ever," I received a telephone call from Frater. His voice was melodic and soothing. He asked if I had heard from Regardie, and if I was aware of what had happened. I told him I had heard from Francis, and that I knew Regardie had dropped the antimony glass temperature-determination project. Frater went on to say how important the project was, telling me of its intended future application, and stated he would, "…have to find someone else to take on the task…" By now I knew about his sly ways, and replied,

"I wish I knew someone who could help, Frater. I have my hands so full though, I couldn't even think of taking it on myself. Maybe you could pull one of your employees at Paralab, maybe the Lab Director, and have him do it? With his B.Sc. in Chemistry, I'm sure he could do the work for you. Have you thought of that?"

There was a pause followed by, "We'll have to see." Frater never broached the subject with me again. He went on to ask if I too was going to:

"…back out on your promise to do the Water Work and take it to the Homunculus stage? Because if you are, I want to know now. It is a very serious matter that your friend Israel broke his word, and I fear it has caused a tremendous breach between us. I don't know if it can be repaired, and I don't want to be deceived anymore by anyone. There is simply too much at stake! Well, Joe, what are you going to do?"

My former resolve in the conversation weakened, and in German I answered, "I am loyal to the end!" Frater laughed, the sense of ease at having heard this being clear in his voice and replied, "Ich erwartete nicht weniger!" (I did not expect less!) Thus, throughout 1979 and for several years to follow, I continued with the Water Work, as the reader will see in the next chapter.

I never saw the furnace again in any of the PRS labs, or at Paralab. I looked for it and even ask Frater as to its whereabouts during my last class. All he indicated was that it wasn't available, but that they intended to use it in the future. It was then I realized that the furnace and pyrometer—along with Frater's dream of making available the Fixed and Unfixed Tinctures of the Glasses of the Seven Planets of the Ancients—had been shelved, most probably, permanently. This was later corroborated for me by Regardie who brought the matter up in a conversation we had in the Fall of 1982. For in that conversation I found out what had happened to the equipment, at least, where it had been over the past several years. Almost as a passing aside, he mentioned that the furnace remained with him "...until a few months ago..." when "...one of Albert's students from here [California] picked it up and returned with it to PRS. Consider it a valiant effort, Joe, but one that will never see its intended purpose fulfilled! Just write it off and forget about it." Regardie was right.

When Regardie returned to the PRS for his repeated Septa Class in November 1979, he did not stay the full two weeks. On the fifth day of class he returned to his home in California, telling those who asked about his early return, that his girlfriend, Alice, had broken her leg, and he needed to get back to her. Privately, he explained to me that

"...on the fourth night after class he invited me over to his house for a private chat. But I knew him, and so I was wary. I went expecting a confrontation, and that's exactly what I got! When I got there, he jumped all over me! Albert was furious about my 'carelessness' over the 'antimony issue.' He told me not only had I let him down, but also Paralab and its thousands of customers around the world, by not completing the job I promised to do! He told me many were waiting for healing by the tinctures of antimony. And now, depriving

them of these medicaments laid squarely on my shoulders! He shouldn't have said that! To lay all that on me was worse than cruel and criminal! It was the final straw! I told him what I thought of him, his Christian hypocrisy, his laziness by not doing his own work yet demanding it be done by others, his subterfuge in using people such as you and me and God knows how many others because we'll never know, and that I had enough of him, his Paracelsus Research Society, all of it! Emmy tried to calm us down, but we were both too far gone. It turned into such a shouting match! Reminded me of my time with Crowley! I was beside myself! After all I had done for him, for him to have taken that attitude and tone with me was inexcusable! I got up, left their house, packed my things, and was on my way home the next day."

Thus, the stage had been set for the final work I would do for Frater Albertus and the Paracelsus Research Society. The Trinity that had been formed between the three of us ended abruptly. Over the next five years—until Frater's demise in July of 1984—he and Regardie did not communicate. Regardie did receive a letter from Frater, "...sometime in 1982 I think..." as he explained later on, but he said he "...destroyed the letter. I didn't even open it. I wanted no more to do with him. What he was doing was noble and important, yes. I have no doubt about that or the practical laboratory Alchemy he teaches. My problem is with him though, and I can't separate the two. So, I said the hell with it all, and I destroyed the letter without so much as a glance at what it said, and I never heard from him again. I left it at that, and to this day, I'm glad I did." This was according to Regardie as he explained during one of our conversations in February 1985, only one month before his end.

But this did not prevent me from keeping Regardie abreast of what was happening on the Water Work, every step of the way. For he was genuinely interested in the subject, and particularly in its application to the generation of the Homunculus, as was Frater Albertus. In fact, I told Frater that I would continue to inform

Regardie of any experimental progress made in these areas, even though the situation between them was what it was. Frater's reply was short and to the point: "Do what you will." And I did.

Chapter Seven

On the Generation of Animals

From April 1979 onward, I involved myself in the Water Work. The first paper, "The Analytical Technique Applied to the Water Work: A Modern Approach", appeared in Volume 1, Winter, 1980, in the publication of Frater's, *Essential—Journal of Evolutionary Thought in Action*. This was followed by the paper, "On the Generation of Animals", which was published in the Volume 3, Summer, 1982, issue of *Essentia*.

Since the journal, along with the PRS, have been defunct these past twenty-three years, back copies of issues are no longer available. However, PDF copies are being distributed through one of the Yahoo Groups on the web that I accidentally came across, as are *all* of the *Alchemical Laboratory Bulletins* from 1960 through 1972. Nevertheless, to save the reader the interminable task of trying to find these resources on the Web—they are *not* directly listed in any of the search engines—I am giving those papers here, but from my original notes. In fact, the several editorial errors that appeared in their published forms have been corrected here in this current presentation, since the Paracelsus College—the new name for the Paracelsus Research Society which Frater choose in 1980, after the three, Seven Year Cycle of Classes were completed—did not make the corrections I requested. Additionally, I have added commentaries to these new presentations to bring the entire process up to date for the contemporary reader, who may decide to experiment with this material. What is to follow then, is an expanded, updated, and therefore essentially new presentation of those early papers.

❄❄❄❄

The Analytical Technique Applied to the Water Work: A Modern Approach
Joseph C. Lisiewski, Ph.D.

In addition to the artful gleanings which the Alchemical experimentalist has learned to appreciate, the analytical nature of this Science must also be carefully kept in view to fully understand the processes and various manipulative operations which underlie this pursuit. It is essential then, that the modern student pose to every operation the questions:

1. What is to be accomplished in terms of a practical end result?
2. What common factors involved in the experiment can be more efficiently reproduced by modern means?

Of course, the understanding of the theory behind any given operation is a prelude to the above.

As an example of this approach, assume the student is engaged in the production of a functional, permanent Herbal Stone. If he chose to proceed according to the process laid down in *Circulatum Urbigerus*,[1] he would find the first requirement is that of obtaining a sulphureous medium with which to imbibe the salts. Further, it would be apparent that a large quantity of menstruum, greatly reduced in concentration, would result. This, in turn, would require extended periods of imbibition of the salts to bring about the desired

---

[1] B. Urbigerus, *Circulatum Urbigerus,* 1690, Para Publishing Co., Salt Lake City, Utah, 1973, pp. 36–37.

effect. Conversely, through the application of the analytical technique, he would find that through soxhlet extraction, a highly concentrated sulphureous medium would be obtained, not only in a relatively short period of time, but due to its increased concentration would decrease the time necessary for imbibition of the salts to bring about their saturation.

Hence, the knowledge of the theory of each operation, coupled with the application of the analysis, can go far toward the effective utilization of time, while increasing the probability of successful completion.

The Analytical Technique Applied to the Water Work Theory

In the *Golden Chain of Homer,* it states:

Take a quantity of dew, rain, snow or hail if you like; but the most expeditious way is if you can take rainwater from a thunder shower, receive it into clean glazed vessels, and filter it, in order to separate the dirt from it which intermixes from the roofs of houses, and you will, after filtration, have a Clear, Crystalline water, of no particular taste, in fact a fine clear water, fit to be used like any other fine water. Place this collected water in a warm garret, where neither the sun nor moon can shine upon it, cover the vessels with a linen cloth, to prevent the dust from getting into it.

Let it stand a Month unmoved, and if the place is warm enough, you will by this time perceive an alteration in the water, because this water begins by the power of the implanted spirit to grow warm although imperceptibly and to break. It begins to ferment and putrefy and acquires a bad smell, and you will observe that it becomes turbid, although it was perfectly clear at first, and a brown spongy earth ascends swimming at the Top, which increases daily and from its weight falls to the bottom.

Here you see a separation, occasioned by the ingrafted spirit of the gross from the subtle. The separated earth is brown, spongy or like wool, slimy and slippery and this slimy earth is the Universal Gur of Nature.[2]

This Gur, or pre-adamic earth, is the base material from which the three Kingdoms of Nature (*i.e.,* the Mineral, Vegetable and Animal) are created.[3]

Now, the enterprising student who has attended the classes of Alchemical Instruction at the former Paracelsus Research Society (now, the Paracelsus College, Utah Institute of Parachemistry) and desires to reproduce this experiment encounters difficulty when comparing the technique as given in the *Golden Chain of Homer* with the oral instructions delivered at the former Paracelsus Research Society. Specifically, students have been orally instructed to collect rainwater during a violent thunderstorm, but to do so in such a manner that the water so collected does not come in contact with a building or the ground to preserve the water's electrical charge. Yet, the *Golden Chain of Homer* instructs that the water be filtered to remove the dirt which intermixed with it from the roofs of houses. However, by applying the analytical technique, we shall see that the modern oral instructions have their basis in modern day considerations, and as such, are correct. Hence, in using our analytical technique we approach the problem in the following manner. We know from the title page of the present edition that the *Golden Chain of Homer* was first published in Frankfurt and Leipzig in 1723. If we consider the structure of the dwellings of that period, we find they were composed of wood, brick, clay and straw, all of which are excellent insulating materials. In addition, we know that electricity was not yet harnessed, and therefore no electrical wiring

---

[2] H. Nintzel, Compiler, *The Golden Chain of Homer*, 1723, Restoration of Alchemical Manuscripts Society, Richardson, Texas, 1978, pp. 35–36.
[3] Paracelsus Research Society, *Parachemy*, Vol. V, No. 2, p. 429; 1977.

Israel Regardie & the Philosopher's Stone 159

existed in the dwellings. Hence, water collected from such structures retained its electrical charge, and was suitable for this experiment...in that time period.

Today, however, modern construction techniques not only employ electrical wiring for buildings, but grounded electrical connections which earths electrical charges. Rain pipes also are found possessing the same grounding principle, thus directing even minute electrical charges to ground. As a consequence, rainwater collected from buildings in this present day would lack the critical electrical charge component. It is therefore of fundamental importance that rainwater collected for the experiment of the generation of the three Kingdoms through Gur production be collected in vessels completely insulated from any ground connection so as to enable the water to retain its electrical charge.

Our second point of consideration is the purity of the atmosphere at the time when the water is collected, since the air should be as clean and clear as possible.[4] Once again, we must analyze the prevailing circumstances of the time to comply with the principles involved. If we consider the date of 1723, the date of the first publication of the *Golden Chain of Homer,* we find a world largely free of atmospheric contamination. In contrast, our own age is just the opposite. High levels of pollution in our environment have given rise to corresponding protection agencies aimed at rectifying these conditions. In relation to this, we have to consider the phenomena of acid rain. This is a form of pollution resulting from high sulphur burning coal. Specifically, it contaminates rainwater during precipitation, such that the rainwater subsequently received is impure. Therefore, a sample of the collected rainwater should first be filtered and then distilled. If a murky, reddish brown substance remains in the distillation flask, the presence of acid rain can be

---

[4] H. Nintzel, Compiler, *The Golden Chain of Homer,* 1723, Restoration of Alchemical Manuscripts Society, Richardson, Texas, 1978, pp. 35–36.

suspected, requiring all the rainwater to be distilled prior to putrefaction. In this way, a contaminant-free Gur can be assured.

Finally, we have to consider the phenomenon of lightning to understand more fully its role in the process. We know that lightning is an electrostatic phenomenon consisting of electrical discharge between adjacent clouds or between clouds and ground.[5] And while the physics of lightning and its effects on rainwater are complex, the general consensus of alchemical theory on the subject requires its effects to produce a Gur which can be used to generate the three Kingdoms. Thus, if acid rain is detected requiring distillation prior to putrefaction, then high speed water distillers are called for which, due to their metallic construction and grounded electrical features, will negate the electrical charge. When such is found to be the case, or if it is desired to increase the electrical component of the water, then the phenomenon of lightning must be simulated. Such simulation can be achieved through the use of a Van de Graaff generator. This is an electrostatic device which produces high voltage electrical power through the interaction of electric fields, and is easily adaptable to electrifying water.

Experimental Procedure

I. Component preparation

Using our analysis thus far we have seen that it is necessary that the rainwater used for the generation of the three Kingdoms be collected directly from the sky. Further, due to atmospheric pollution, acid which can exist in the collected rainwater must be removed through distillation in order to achieve a contaminant-free Gur.

Finally, when modern high-speed water distillation techniques are used, negation of the water's electrical charge component can

---

[5] "Lightning," *Encyclopedia Britannica*, 15th ed., Vol. X, pp. 966–968.

result. However, through electrostatic electrification as produced by a Van de Graaff, the charge can be replaced. To comply with this criterion, the following methods and procedures were used:

A. Water Collection—Polyethylene sheeting available from most department and hardware stores can be used to construct a receiving vessel. The author used a section $12' \times 100'$ suspended between wooden slats to construct a 1200-square-foot receptacle. During a violent electrical thunderstorm lasting only 45 minutes, 125 gallons of rainwater was collected.

B. Purification—The rainwater was checked for acid contamination by distilling a 500 ml sample in a conventional distillation train. While the distillate was clear, the residue remaining in the distillation flask was murky, and reddish in color. Subsequent analysis by chromatographic techniques showed the presence of nitrates, sulphates, and a mixture of generally acidic components, thus establishing the presence of acid rain. Quantitative analysis showed concentrations as high as 0.05 grams per liter, a relatively high concentration which would adversely affect the purity of the Gur. Hence, the entire 125 gallons of rainwater were distilled using a high-speed steam distiller, which produced 11 gallons of distilled water per 24-hour period. In less than 12 days, the entire quantity of water was distilled, thereby eliminating the prohibitively long and tedious process encountered with conventional distillation trains.

C. Electrification—As previously mentioned, the use of typical high-speed steam distillers can result in the negation of the electrical charge component of the water. The charge can be introduced through electrostatic electrification as produced by a Van de Graaff. (In the absence of acid rain where prior distillation is not required, this technique can be used to strengthen the water's existing charge.) The author used a 500,000 volt at 50 microampere unit to electrify the water over a 12-hour period. This was accomplished by connecting a platinum electrode from the charged sphere of the Van de Graaff generator directly to the water. In this way, a concentrated simulation of lightning phenomena results in a highly charged water medium. Such Van de Graaff generators can be purchased in kit form from scientific supply houses for $100 to $200.

Commentary—Van de Graaff generators have risen dramatically in price. Today, a unit comparable to the one cited here costs between $500–$1,100. I do not recommend anyone attempting to build such a device from a kit as I did. Motor-matching, along with speed regulation of the motor shaft and belt assembly are tricky, as is obtaining a symmetrical charge distribution over the surface of the generator's electrified sphere: it is necessary to properly position the electrical contact brushes. Frater Albertus found this to be the case, as will be dealt with in the closing remarks of this chapter. Those interested in this work should buy the unit assembled and tested.

II. Gur production

125 gallons of the distilled and electrified rainwater was placed in 10 plastic food grade containers, each with a capacity of 15 gallons. Two controls were also established, as follows:

Control 1 – 10 gallons of rainwater collected from the roof of a house. This was filtered, but not electrified.

Control 2 – 10 gallons of rainwater collected from the roof. It was filtered and electrified as previously described.

All containers were covered with a finely porous percale material, and set aside in a dark place at 75–85° F. for 90 days to putrefy. At the end of 90 days, the containers were opened and the results analyzed. The 10 containers which had been distilled and electrified showed a **39%** per container higher yield of Gur when compared to Control 2, and a **51%** higher yield per container when compared to Control 1. In addition, the Gur obtained through distillation and electrification had a much deeper reddish color to it, as well as a highly repetitive matrix structure. The Gur from Controls 1 and 2 lacked these properties.

Commentary—*Great care must be taken to insure the containers and percale material are not contaminated. Carefully wiping the containers with 70% rubbing alcohol ensures their sterility. Allow the alcohol to dry thoroughly however, before adding the water. The percale material should be washed in a weak solution of bleach and left to air dry in a clean environment. These small measures can ensure the integrity of one's experiments in this work.*

Finally, the Gur obtained from Controls 1 and 2 showed the presence of acidic components when analyzed by chromatographic techniques, thus establishing the carry through of the acids to the Gur formation.

Conclusion

It has been shown that through distillation, acidic components present in rainwater should be eliminated prior to putrefaction to obtain a pure Gur. Further, electrostatic electrification of this distilled rainwater prior to putrefaction not only results in a higher yield of Gur, but in a highly-ordered structural arrangement of the substance.

Commentary—*Further work with the Gur showed it to possess an* orthorhombic *structure, with a melting point of 36.4 degrees Centigrade.*

It is up to the enterprising experimentalist to establish the relevancy of these techniques in his own generation of the three Kingdoms.

On the Generation of Animals
Joseph C. Lisiewski, Ph.D.

In the article entitled "The Analytical Technique Applied to the Water Work: A Modern Approach,"[6] the objectives were to:

1. Confirm the existence of the substance termed Gur as delineated in the *Golden Chain of Homer*.[7]
2. Present the physical characteristics of this substance.
3. Evaluate the role of electrical phenomena in relationship to the production and structure of the Gur.
4. Define the variables that effect the production of this substance as a function of modern times.

While these objectives were being met, they were preliminary to further experimentation along the guidelines as established in the *Golden Chain of Homer,* and expanded upon by oral instructions given at the Paracelsus College, Utah Institute of Parachemistry (formerly the Paracelsus Research Society).

The text cited and instructions given deal with the generation of the three Kingdoms of Nature, *i.e.,* the Animal, Vegetable, and Mineral. These Kingdoms can be generated in a somewhat artificial manner through imbibition of the substance termed Gur, or Preadamic Earth as it is also termed[8] with various combinations of water from which it is derived. The writer's interest lies exclusively in the generation of the Animal Kingdom, and it is to this extent that the experiments in this second phase of laboratory research were confined.

---

[6] Paracelsus College, *Essentia,* Vol. 1. Winter 1980, p. 6–7, 10.
[7] H. Nintzel, Compiler, *The Golden Chain of Homer,* 1723, Restoration of Alchemical Manuscripts Society, Richardson, Texas 1978.
[8] Paracelsus Research Society, *Parachemy,* Vol. V, No. 2, p. 29, 1977.

A total of 37 experiments, conducted over a 3-year period, were attempted. Success came on the 35th, 36th and 37th undertaking. While the number of variables is admittedly enormous, in the end, analysis offered a workable combination. The results are *miniature* animal-like organisms.

The purpose of this present paper is to explain fully and in complete detail the methods used: those which brought success as well as those which ended in failure. In Science, failure can teach as much, if not more, than success.

Since this is the second phase of the experiment, it seems a brief review of the first article, "The Analytical Technique Applied to the Water Work: A Modern Approach" is desirable. Without being repetitious, this review is intended to provide present readers [the previous paper was published in 1980; this paper appeared 2 years later] without access to its original format with key points of explanation, as well as provide a composite whole of the experiment between two covers.

❄❄❄❄

THE ANALYTICAL TECHNIQUE APPLIED TO THE WATER WORK—A REVIEW

In any scientific presentation, exact reference points must be provided to allow accurate evaluation of the methods, variables, and conclusions drawn. To this end, the methods of water collection and preparation as laid down in the *Golden Chain of Homer* are quoted here:

Take a quantity of dew, rain, snow or hail which you like; but the most expeditious way is if you can take rainwater from a thunder shower, receive it into clean glazed vessels, and filter it, in order to separate the dirt from it which intermixes from the roofs of houses, and you will, after filtration, have a Clear, Crystalline water, of no particular taste, in fact a fine clear water, fit to be used like any other fine water. Place this collected water in a warm garret, where neither the sun nor moon can shine upon it, cover the vessels with a linen cloth, to prevent the dust from getting into it.

Let it stand a Month unmoved, and if the place is warm enough, you will by this time receive an alteration in the water, because this water begins by the power of the implanted spirit to grow warm although imperceptibly and to break; it begins to ferment and putrefy and acquires a bad smell, and you will observe that it becomes turbid, although it was perfectly clear at first, and a brown spongy earth ascends swimming at the top, which increases daily and from its weight falls to the bottom.

Here you see a separation, occasioned by the ingrafted spirit of the gross from the subtle. The separated earth is brown, spongy or like wool, slimy and slippery and this slimy earth is the Universal Gur of Nature.[9]

This Gur, of Preadamic Earth, is the base material from which the three Kingdoms of Nature are generated.[10]

I. Water Collection

The practical application of this is the collection of the rainwater as the first step. This was accomplished using a section of 12´×100´ of polyethylene sheeting, suspended between wooden slats. This resulted in a 1200 square foot receptacle. During a violent electrical thunderstorm, a total of 125 gallons of rainwater was collected. Although the second step would normally be filtration followed by putrefaction, the rainwater was filtered and checked for acid contamination by distilling a 500 ml sample in a conventional

---

[9] H. Nintzel, Compiler, *The Golden Chain of Homer*, 1723, Restoration of Alchemical Manuscripts Society, Richardson, Texas 1978, pp. 35–36.
[10] Paracelsus Research Society, *Parachemy*, Vol. V, No. 2, p. 429, 1977.

distillation train. (This procedure was introduced due to current high levels of acid rain which are prevalent throughout most of this country.) While the distillate was clear, the residue remaining in the distillation flask was a murky yellowish to reddish color. Subsequent analysis by chromatographic techniques showed an admixture of nitrates, sulphates, and a mixture of generally acidic components, thus establishing the presence of acid rain. Quantitative analysis of the contaminant yielded a concentration of 0.05 grams per liter, a relatively high concentration which could adversely affect the purity of the Gur. Hence, it became necessary to distill all the rainwater prior to putrefaction. However, since the classical distillation train method is prohibitively extensive in terms of time and economy, a high-speed steam distiller was used. This device, which is capable of producing 11 gallons of highly purified distilled water in a 24-hour period, completed the task in less than 12 days.

II. Water Re-Electrification

The second factor of consideration is the electrification of the water. As stated in the *Golden Chain of Homer,* the rainwater is to be collected during an electrical thunderstorm, the natural electrical phenomena adding an electrical charge and high niter content to the water. However, due to the metallic construction of the high-speed steam distiller (common to all makes and brands), as well as their grounded electrical features, negation of the electrical charge component can result. As such, it became necessary to re-introduce that charge. The mode of re-electrification chosen was electrostatic electrification as produced by a Van de Graaff generator. This is a device which produces high voltage electrical energy through the interaction of electric fields. The unit here was rated at 500,000 volts at 50 microamperes. It is easily adaptable to electrifying water by the simple expedient of attaching a platinum electrode from the charged sphere directly to the water. The water is then electrified over a 12-hour period.

III. Gur production

The entire quantity of distilled and re-electrified rainwater was placed in 10 plastic food grade containers, each with a capacity of 15 gallons. Two controls were established, as follows:

Control 1 – 10 gallons of rainwater collected from the roof of a house. It was filtered but not electrified.

Control 2 – 10 gallons of rainwater collected from the roof of a house. It was filtered and electrified.

All containers were covered with a finely porous percale material and set aside in a dark place at 75–80° F. for 90 days to putrefy, although 30 days to 45 days will do as well.

At the end of 90 days, the containers were opened and the results analyzed. The 10 containers which had been distilled and re-electrified showed a **39%** per container higher yield of Gur when compared to Control 2, and a **51%** higher yield per container when compared to Control 1. In addition, the Gur obtained through distillation and re-electrification had a much deeper reddish color, as well as a highly repetitive matrix structure. The Gur from Controls 1 and 2 lacked these properties. In addition, the Gur from Controls 1 and 2 showed the presence of acidic components when analyzed by chromatographic methods, thus establishing the carry-through of the acids to the Gur formation.

IV. Conclusion

It has been shown that rainwater available today is highly likely to contain acid components due to industrial processes. As such, it must first be distilled prior to putrefaction. The electrical charge component must then be re-introduced, either by the means given, or similar means. Putrefaction in a warm, dark place follows next, which yields a highly turbid condition in the water. The final step is the distillation of the water which separates the Gur from them.

We now enter the second phase of the experiment: the generation of the Animal Kingdom of Nature Proper.

❄❄❄❄

ON THE GENERATION OF ANIMALS

I. Experimental Procedure — Evaluation of the Method used in Animal Generation according to the *Golden Chain of Homer*.

A. Water Separation

Once again it is necessary to establish our reference points by quoting from the *Golden Chain of Homer*:

Now pour your troubled Water and Earth into a large glass body which is placed in an earthen pot, fixed into a charcoal distilling furnace, apply a large alembic and receiver and light your fire, which keep so gentle that only the Steam or Vapours rise. Let this all come over first as a pure water, which contains animated Air, that is, Air and Fire. Distill no more of this very volatile water over, than what will go over with the gentlest degree of Heat, whilst the subject in the body only vapours away but must not be suffered to boil; in this manner you vapour over about the ¼ part of the whole or less.

Take the receiver off with this Very volatile water; This water, the more so, if you afterwards rectify it per se over a Steam Bath, is more luminous and clearer than common distilled water, which is proof that it contains much Air and Fire.

Now apply another receiver and continue the distillation raising your heat sufficiently, so as to cause the thickest water in the glass body to boil, and in this manner you must distill all the water over, which will appear like water and in drops in the alembic; continue the distillation until it remains in the body like melted honey and looks brown, but beware of distilling until it remains dry, because you would burn the young and tender Virgin Earth in the bottom of the Vessel, which is not yet fixed. Take the distilled water away and put it by as the Element Earth.

The honey like matter or the moist Earth remaining in the glass body take out cleanly and put it into a china basin and set it in the Sun to evaporate until it is perfectly dry; then grind it in a glass mortar to a subtil Earth, now you have Separated the Elements out of your chaos.

Now it remains to be proved that they are truly Elements, or else it must be false what I have written, that all sublunary subjects proceed from them. To produce heavenly subjects out of this chaos or Metheors, as this water itself is a Methorical production, let no one undertake; but we will demonstrate that animals, vegetables, and minerals may and can be generated, and that is what we pretend and no further.[11]

There are several points discussed in the manuscript which require further elucidation. The following should clarify the process, such that its reproduction in the laboratory will be more profitable.

1. The ¼ part of the water which is to be collected by the gentlest degree of heat should be kept at 95–98° C. Upon even heating of the distillation train, a "sweat," *i.e.*, water distillation without boiling, will result. A good quality, calibrated thermometer is essential.

2. The first ¼ part is termed the Water of Fire and Air, but appears in parts of the manuscript as simply the Water of Air. It must be remembered that when the term Water of Air is encountered, a Water of Fire and Air Combination is actually indicated.

3. The second ¾ part is the Water of Water, and should be distilled over by rapid boiling, but not too vigorously. A temperature of **100–102° C** will accomplish this without burning the Gur.

---

[11] H. Nintzel, Compiler, *The Golden Chain of Homer*, 1723, Restoration of Alchemical Manuscripts Society, Richardson, Texas 1978, pp. 36–38.

4. After distilling over the second ¾ part of water, immediately pour the reddish-brown liquid (which contains the Gur) left in the distillation flask into a narrow porcelain container, the bottom of which should have as small a surface area as possible. Next, place the container and contents in a sand bath at 75–80° F. to dry gently. (Containers with a large surface area tend to disperse the Gur so thinly, that the heat of drying, even though gently, will cause it to burn.) With the narrow container, the resulting Gur will be powdery and reddish in color.

a. Water Separation and Gur Production

The initial experiment dealt with the separation of the Water of Fire and Air and the Water of Water by distilling 10 liters of putrefied rainwater at any given time through a conventional distillation train. (The conventional distillation train was used at this point due to the continual refluxing of water which high speed steam distillers require. This results in a high degree of uncertainty that the most volatile first ¼ part is truly coming over first.) Heating was accomplished using heating mantles driven by 10 ampere variable transformers, which provide high degrees of regulation.

The first ¼ part, that is, the Water of Fire and Air, collected, measured 2500 ml. Total time of distillation: 88.5 hours. The water was placed in Pyrex flasks, stoppered with a cork stopper to insure lack of contamination due to sulphurated rubber stoppers. The pH of the first ¼ part was 6.99. (All pH measurements were made with a digital electronic pH meter, calibrated against standard reference solutions, and adjusted for slope and temperature conditions.)

The second ¼ part, *i.e.*, the Water of Water, was boiled over at 102° C. and stored in the same manner as the first ¼ part. Its pH was 6.78. The total time of distillation was 12.75 hours. The residue in the distilling flask was poured rapidly into a 250 ml porcelain crucible, and placed in a sand bath at 80° F. Complete drying occurred in 18 hours. From this, 4.85 grams of reddish, powdery Gur was received. It was finely ground, and prepared for electron bombardment.

In any experiment such as this, it can be argued that bacteria, spore, or larvae present in the putrefied and distilled water could account for positive results. And rightly so. Therefore, a means of sterilization of the Gur was necessary. Electron bombardment was chosen due to its effectiveness in destroying the organisms mentioned. Essentially, the Gur was placed in a Pyrex vessel, evacuated to 27″ Hg continuous, with the vacuum pump having a CFM at 0″ Hg of 4.0. The electronic and vacuum jet were connected to the vessel by ground glass joints, and sealed with high vacuum grease. 50,000 volts at 25 microamperes was applied for 6 hours.

Finally, the Gur was added to a watchglass which was previously sterilized by autoclaving.

b. Animal Generation According to the Golden Chain of Homer

To give a complete rendition of the procedure as laid down in the *Golden Chain of Homer,* an exact quote is necessary:

Take your before mentioned dried and powdered Earth, pour first together 1 part of Water and 3 parts of Air, with this mixture humect your Earth so copiously that it may become like liquid or melted honey, place the glass body which contains this mixture on the air, where it is warm the sun may shine on it but not too hot, nor at the meridian, and the glass is left open.

You will perceive that in a few days, there will be different kinds of small vermine in the thick water; when the water diminishes and dries up, you must humect it again, so that it may remain of the same consistence like syrup, as before; and you will perceive that the first small vermine will and loose themselves, and others will be produced who will feed on their putrefaction, and become larger and more in number.[12]

---

[12] H. Nintzel, Compiler, *The Golden Chain of Homer,* 1723, Restoration of Alchemical Manuscripts Society, Richardson, Texas 1978, p. 39.

To comply with that which is given, 1 part of the second ¾ and 3 parts of the first ¼ were combined and used to imbibe the Gur in an open-air condition in the laboratory. (Although this would seem to negate the sterilization procedures carried out previously, we shall see later through additional controls this was not the case.) The technique of imbibition is such that the Gur must maintain a honey-like consistency. This poses a practical problem in that the Gur, once imbibed, must not be allowed to dry out, lest the imbibition cycle be started over again. This necessitates careful observation of the process. (Through experimentation however, it was found that 1 gram of Gur could be brought to this honey-like consistency by imbibing **5.5 ml** of the water mixture. At an average room temperature of 70° F. the Gur will dry out in 65 minutes, thereby requiring re-imbibition every 50 minutes to prevent this.) The watchglass and contents were kept in indirect sunlight for 72 hours, while the consistency was maintained.

The result of the experiment: negative. Neither living organisms on the surface nor beneath it could be detected. This basic procedure was conducted 10 times. Each time, the results were negative. In an attempt to isolate possible variables, water was procured from various parts of the country, and the process conducted an additional 15 times, each time analyzing and changing such factors as temperatures of distillation, lengthening and shortening times of imbibition, varying drying procedures, *etc.* All results were negative.

c. Conclusion

From the numerous experiments conducted, it was concluded that modern atmospheric conditions causing acid rain, and/or the means used to rectify the waters' conditions negated the experiments. Hence, it became necessary to investigate other variations of the process of Animal generation.

II. The Analytical Experimental Approach

Upon analysis, the variables which presented themselves for further consideration were:

A. Water transformation through acid contamination.
B. High speed steam distillation of the water.
C. Re-electrification of the distilled water prior to putrefaction.

In an effort to test these variables, two additional experiments in each category were run. In category A. rainwater with an acid component and a pH of 4.95 was filtered but not distilled, or re-electrified. After putrefaction, its pH was 5.02. The waters were separated, Gur obtained and sterilized by electron bombardment, and imbibed. Results: negative. In category B., rainwater with a pH of 4.87 was distilled by high speed techniques, resulting in a pH of 5.20. After re-electrification, it was putrefied, and yielded a pH of 5.31. Gur was obtained, sterilized, and imbibed. Results: negative.

In category C., the experiments were divided into 2 parts: C.1. Rainwater, pH 4.87 was filtered, distilled by a conventional distillation train, which yielded a pH of 5.05. It was not electrified. In C.2., rainwater was filtered, distilled by high speed techniques, electrified, and re-distilled by conventional distillation train. It yielded a pH of 5.41. Both waters, when putrefied, yielded a pH of 5.22. Again, waters were separated, and the Gur obtained, sterilized, and imbibed. Results: negative.

Conclusion

The experimental variations seemed to indicate that these variables were of no import in contributing to the negative results. Rather, it seemed that the process as interpreted in the *Golden Chain of Homer* should be suspect.

III. The Analytical Experimental Approach — *Process Review*

At this juncture, the *Golden Chain of Homer* was reviewed, in an effort to find something which may have been overlooked. One point, concerning the re-distillation of the first ¼ part, to bring about increased "luminosity" was considered.

In this attempt, 10 liters of rain water, (pH 9.2) was filtered, distilled by high-speed techniques, electrified, and resulted in a pH of 5.25. Upon putrefaction, it gave a pH of 5.53. The Waters were separated. The first ¼ part yielded a pH of 6.82. The second ¾ part gave a pH of 6.96. However, while distilling the first ¼ part, it was noticed that the pH of the first ½ of the first ¼ part gave a pH of 5.50, *i.e.*, near that of the original putrefied water. The second ½ of the first ¼ gave a pH of 8.16. This interesting development prompted the labeling of the first ½ of the first ¼ part as the Water of Fire, and the second ½ of the first ¼ part as the Water of Air, due to volatility considerations. The second ¾ part was not re-distilled; its pH was 6.96.

The Gur was prepared as in all previous cases, and imbibed. This time however, the 3 parts of the Water of Fire and Air were produced by combining 1.5 parts of the separated Water of Fire with 1.5 parts of the Water of Air, to the standard 1 part of the Water of Water (the second ¾ part), to give the final 3:1 ratio. After 72 hours of imbibition, the results were negative. The experiment was conducted a second time, with the same results.

Referring once again to the *Golden Chain of Homer,* a statement was seen in a new light: ***"Let it all come over first as a pure water, which contains animated Air, that is Air and Fire.***"[13] In keeping with this, the 34th experiment was run by sweating over 9.8 liters after standard procedures of preparation of the 10-liter quantity of putrefied water, whose pH was 5.56. After separation, the pH of the first ½ of the first ¼, the second ½ of the first ¼, and the second ¾, were approximately as those in the last experiment. The residue in the flask after first sweating the 9.8 liters over was judged to be meaningless, and disregarded. The Gur was prepared by electron

---

[13] H. Nintzel, Compiler, *The Golden Chain of Homer,* 1723, Restoration of Alchemical Manuscripts Society, Richardson, Texas 1978, p. 36.

bombardment; the 3:1 water ratio was produced as in the last experiment, and the Gur imbibed. After 80 hours, the results were negative.

In the 35th experiment, the residue left in the distillation flask after sweating 9.8 liters of the water over was dried in standard fashion and added to the Gur that was obtained after separation of the water, which was conducted in precisely the same manner as given for the last experiment. pH measurements of the first halves and second ¾, again, were approximately as those in the previous two experiments. The Gur was sterilized and the water mixture produced again as in the previous two experiments, and the Gur imbibed over an 80-hour period. Results: Something entirely different occurred this time. Visual observation showed the presence of 2 miniature worm-like organisms in the Gur. One possessed little motion, and kept mostly beneath the surface, while the second, a much lighter brown in color than its viscous surroundings, moved in and out of the Gur freely. No more than 2 organisms were detected throughout an intensive period of observation.

After 32 hours, the Gur was allowed to dry out, and was then re-imbibed to test for regeneration, but in larger form, as stated in the *Golden Chain of Homer*. An additional 80 hours of re-imbibition yielded negative results: the organisms did not regenerate.

The 36th experiment, conducted precisely as the last, yielded 2 organisms also, both quite rapid in movement. When placed under a microscope, individual details of their structure were ill defined due to their body densities. One feature that did stand out was an elongated body with 4 tentacle-like projections, *i.e.*, 2 at each end. Upon return to their environment, the Gur was dried out and re-imbibed. No new, larger generations were detected. At the same time, 4 other trays of Gur, imbibed with the first ½ of the first ¼ of water, the second of the first ¼, and the second ¾ of water, and an original mixture of the combined 3 parts of the Water of Air and Fire (unseparated), respectively, were imbibed at the same time and exposed to the same environmental conditions. These controls gave negative results, thus verifying the positive results received were not due to contamination. The 37th experiment took place using the same controls, plus two others: one watchglass of Gur was distilled rainwater, the other with tap water. All six controls gave negative results, while the main experiment, repeated exactly as the 35th and 36th, brought forth organisms, although no more than 3 were detected. Upon drying out and re-imbibing, no regeneration occurred.

Conclusion

The fundamental purpose of these experiments was to test the thesis of animal generation as originally set down in the *Golden Chain of Homer*. Extensive experimentation has shown that the core of the thesis is correct, although the process differs. That is where the analytical technique, as exemplified by scientific procedure, demonstrates its essential role in furthering the goals of the experimentalist.

It is hoped that readers of this paper will undertake this pursuit as outlined. Independent confirmation is not only desirable, it is essential.

❄❄❄❄

Prior to publishing these papers in *Essentia,* I discussed them with Regardie and Frater Albertus. While the latter took them in stride with an, oh, yes, of course attitude, Regardie found them fascinating. He wanted to attempt the work himself, owing to its possible implications for creating the Homunculus. However, the amount of equipment required, its high voltage electrical nature, as well as the time and energy commitment, finally dissuaded him from doing so. In fact, after the paper, "On the Generation of Animals" appeared in the Fall of 1982, Regardie had spent some serious money in preparation of replicating my experimental work. But a nasty, although harmless, shock from his Van de Graaff ended his sojourn into this realm of alchemical work. (A Van de Graaff produces extremely low current electrostatic charges that do provide quite a shock, especially when one comes into contact with an earth ground. Such shocks are generally harmless, unless one has a heart condition, in which case it can stop the heart.)

To the best of my knowledge Frater Albertus did not do anything with the scientific data I obtained from these experiments. Nor did he utilize the 'modified' Homeric process I had found to be the case in generating these miniature creatures. This, even though I purchased a second Van de Graaff generator in kit form at his request, and donated it to the newly named, "Paracelsus College, Utah Institute of Parachemistry." For immediately after I obtained my experimental Homeric results, Frater told me he wanted to have "...some of my people reproduce your work. We could stand to study this process in even greater detail..." And so, the generator was purchased and sent to him.

However, after receiving it and building it from the kit, he told me, "...we could not get the generator assembly to work correctly. Some 'electrical thing' I think they told me was giving them problems." As with the case of the furnace and its optical measuring device, I never saw the Van de Graaff again. When I told Regardie he only laughed and said, "Albert will never change. One big time idea after another, and always at someone else's expense!" Nevertheless, Frater did strongly encourage me to continue the work on the Homunculus, which I indeed undertook. Because by that time, after having experienced success in generating these miniature Homerian creatures, I was hell-bent on taking this work as far as I could. And that meant in experimenting with the Homunculus itself. That matter can now be dealt with properly in the next chapter.

Chapter Eight

On the Experimental Aspects of the Homunculus

In May of 1982 I began work on the Homunculus. Before entering into a general outline of the process by which it is possible to create such an 'artificial creature,' it is necessary that a clear understanding is had by the reader of just what the legendary Homunculus truly is, and how that compares to that which I managed to generate in the laboratory. This, although I was not able to take the process to its final conclusion and for the reasons discussed.

(Note: The rendition given below arises from many sources, including the *Encyclopedia Britannica, Wikipedia,* the writings of Paracelsus, some old notes I made on the subject many years ago, as well as my own experimentally-derived knowledge of this creature. Thus, while it is impossible to cite specific sources, the reader will have at least some idea of where this information arose, should one choose to pursue the theoretical investigation of this matter further.)

The concept of the **homunculus** arises from the Latin diminutive of homin-, or homo, meaning, "little man." Its earliest use in literature occurring was circa 1525, according to some authorities. In its plural form, homunculi, it is often used to illustrate the functioning of a system—that is, as a human system, or one in which a complete, functioning human being is the representative outcome. The importance of this latter classification is an end process rather than a beginning concept, in that early elements of such speculations were used to create the concept of the Homunculus.

The idea of this 'little man' is the product of early speculations and theorizing about the nature of sexual reproduction and heredity. It was the early Greeks—most notably, Hippocrates (circa 460–circa 377 B.C.E.), a Greek physician considered to be the father of medicine—who seriously pondered both of these biological issues to further understand not only the reproductive process, but the transmission of physical and even personality characteristics from parent to child. Eventually, through his influence and the school of medicine he founded, a theory termed "Pangenesis" was formulated. This was a view which claimed that sex involved the transfer of miniaturized body parts, (bones, eyes, etc.), albeit invisible in their initial state since their particle-like nature is so small. That is, the essential elements that go into producing a complete human being are invisible to the naked eye of an observer, but nevertheless present in the male sperm. While growing, they separate from each other throughout the gestation period, thereby producing a fully formed baby at birth. This idea was held as being the most reasonable for over eighteen hundred years, having lost favor during the middle of the Renaissance Period. It did enjoy a brief revival however, when Charles Darwin, desperate to support his theory of evolution by natural selection with a viable hypothesis of inheritance, put forward a modified version of Pangenesis in the second half of the nineteenth century.

In Darwin's interpretation, every organ of the body contributed circulating particles called "gemmules," that accumulated in the sex organs; and it was these particles that were ultimately exchanged in the course of sexual reproduction. Since these gemmules were produced throughout an organism's lifetime, it led Darwin to argue that this continuous process of gemmule production allowed any change that occurred in the individual after its birth—as in the case of the stretch of a giraffe's neck imparted by craning for the highest foliage—to be passed on to the next generation. Ironically, to fortify his theory of natural selection further, Darwin also championed certain aspects of Jean-Baptiste Lamarck's theory. In actuality however, Darwin's evolutionary ideas discredited Lamarck's theory of the inheritance of acquired characteristics. However, since Darwin used only particular aspects of Lamarck's theory of inheritance, he continued to believe that natural selection was the driving force behind evolution but supposed that natural selection operated on a variation produced by Pangenesis. It is not difficult to see how such ideas as gemmules, invisible and later miniature body parts, gave rise to the idea of a 'little man,' especially in the occult and alchemical circles that were so universally active during the Renaissance and later periods. For the very fabric of such investigations dealt with the study and experimentation of the hidden aspects of nature, and of their extensions into magical rites and alchemical procedures.

These occult ideas—having been initially fired by the Pangenesis view that embryos were assembled from a set of minuscule components—were further fueled by yet another approach: that of "Pre-Formationism." In this view, the process of assembly was eliminated, with no need for such a mechanical process since the egg or sperm—and exactly which was an extremely contested issue—contained a complete pre-formed individual that was actually referred to as a "Homunculus." Development would simply be a matter of enlarging the Homunculus into a fully formed, independent being. Under this theory of Pre-Formationism, phenomena now attributable to genetic disease was seen as being due to any number of factors, such as: manifestations of God's fury, the malignant influence of demons, intervention by the devil himself, an excess of the father's seed or even a deficiency of it, or punishment for evil or sensual thoughts and feelings on the part of the mother during her pregnancy. In fact, the idea that fetal malformation could occur as a result of a pregnant mother's desires being unfulfilled was so prevalent during the eighteenth century, and the fear so great that her emotions would leave her so stressed and frustrated that a birth defect would occur, Napoleon Bonaparte passed a law in France permitting expectant mothers to shoplift! Such were the consequences of Pre-Formationism, and the early, unenlightened and unscientific views that served to fulfill people's longings for some type of explanation of the universe in which they lived.

Perhaps the greatest authority on the Homunculus is none other than Philippus Aureolus Theophrastus Bombastus Paracelsus von Hohenheim, a Swiss-born alchemist and physician who wrote under the name Paracelsus. He not only believed that diseases were due to specific entities and not humours—the latter being the prevailing view of his day—but that as entities, they could be successfully treated and subsequently cured by specific remedies. This was his contribution to medicine. Alchemically however, he delved into many arcane areas of the field, as a study of his classic tome, *Hermetic and Alchemical Writings of Paracelsus the Great* clearly illustrates. (A.E. Waite edition, Kessinger Publishing.)

One of the arcane areas of alchemy about which he wrote was that of the Homunculus. While his writings appear to be cryptic and delusional, they are only that way to those who have not been trained in the Science and Art that Alchemy truly is. As the reader will see later on in this chapter, my personal experimentation in generating this creature confirmed the essence of Paracelsus' instructions; this, by producing something very real and very physical in the laboratory. It was this that so intrigued both Regardie and Frater Albertus, both of whom shared in my experimental results.

According to Paracelsus, one needed a "spagyric" substance to produce the Homunculus. Typically, encyclopedias and alchemical sources state that this "spagyric" material, a term most probably invented by Paracelsus himself, referred to an alchemical process in which semen or the male sperm was used to bring the Homunculus into existence. It is interesting that they make this assignment to the word as we shall soon see. Further, as the process of the creation of the Homunculus is discussed, the reader will also come to understand the accuracy and importance of the term Spagyrics, and how it applies to the Homunculus, as the word is typically understood. That is, the term is derived from the Greek, "Spao" meaning to separate, and "Ageiro," to combine. In its common usage however, it refers to a type of chemistry that deals with the preparations of medicines—primarily tinctures and extracts—taken from herbal, animal, and mineral substances.

This Paracelsian-defined spagyric substance was to be placed into a glass container. The container was to be sealed and buried in horse dung for a period of forty days, during which the alchemical process of 'digestion' would take place. At the end of the forty-day period, something would be found that would be both alive and would move in the container. Paracelsus stated that at times this would be a man, a Homunculus, but one who had no body and indeed was transparent at that time.

Paracelsus then goes on to state that regardless of these conditions, the creature exists, and it only remains for the Alchemist but to bring him up, a process that is no more difficult than that which was used to generate him. This 'raising process' may be accomplished by feeding the creature daily, over a period of 40 weeks, with the "Arcanum" of human blood. Throughout this time, the forming creature must not be removed from the dung hill in which he was formed. At the end of this time, one will find a living child, as well proportioned as any infant born of a human woman. He will be smaller and more frail than a normal human child though, and will require more care and attention in his education, with physical education being stressed. Some reports state that the creature—even when grown to maturity—will never grow to a height of more than twelve inches.

Other sources relate that the Homunculus has Golem-like propensities, displaying an absolute will of its own, which can manifest suddenly and take its creator by surprise. This surprise manifested by the creature would entail turning on its creator in an attempt to destroy him, after which it escapes its laboratory confines to live a life of its own. In this way, such a being can be said to have Frankenstein-like attributions, although it differs from the Mary Shelly creature in that it pretends to be mentally deficient, all the while plotting and planning against its creator. Highly romantic and stylized? Yes. Still, there are such cautions in older occult literature.

There are other accounts by which such a creature can be brought forth into the world of men. In one of those accounts, the alchemist can make use of the root called Mandrake. It is said that this plant grows where semen—ejaculated by a hanged man during his last convulsive spasms prior to death—drips to the ground and 'fertilizes' the roots of the Mandrake plant which then takes on a vague resemblance to a human figure. The root is to be picked from the earth on a Friday morning before dawn by a black dog, then washed and 'fed' with milk and honey—or in some accounts with human blood—whereupon it will fully develop into a miniature human who will guard and protect its owner.

A third method, recorded during the 18th century by Dr. David Christianus of the University of Giessen, states that the alchemical experimentalist is to take an egg laid by a black hen, punch a tiny hole in the shell, and replace a "...bean-sized portion of the white with human semen." The opening was to be sealed with virgin parchment, and the whole buried in dung on the first day of the March lunar cycle. According to Christianus, a miniature humanoid-figure would emerge from the egg after thirty days. As with the Mandrake-Homunculus, this creature would protect its creator. However, this particular creation would also help its creator in whatever ways the latter wished, providing it was fed a steady diet of lavender seeds and earthworms.

To be sure, there are other accounts of the Homunculus given throughout Medieval and Renaissance literature, not to mention the modern-day accounts of Carl Jung and his interpretation of this idea

Israel Regardie & the Philosopher's Stone 185

in terms of psychoanalysis. But for our purposes, what has been given here should suffice in providing a basic grasp of the manner in which such a creature can allegedly be generated, its behavioral inclinations, and its physical constitution. Is it any wonder that the prospect for actually bringing such a living thing into existence so fascinated Regardie, Frater Albertus, and myself?

In May of 1982 I began the work on the Homunculus. Since the *Generation* paper for Frater's journal was nearly finished, I naturally turned my attention to this final effort of the Water Work right away. But there were several fundamental questions that had to be answered before the experimental work could begin. It was time then, nearly four years after that late-night private discussion Frater had with me in the laboratory, that those questions be addressed. But first, I wanted Regardie's input, since he was deeply interested in this subject. When I brought the issue up to him, his attitude toward it was bittersweet.

I detected his frustration at not being able to engage in such experimental work himself, and yet, at the same time, his desire to be filled in on every part of the process—if indeed, it could be done at all. I got the very distinct impression he was trying to relate the idea of the Homunculus to some type of closely guarded magical work, and so asked him if this was the reason for his interest and the feelings I detected from him during our lengthy discussions on this issue. In a very thoughtful way, as if being careful of what he said and the manner in which he said it, he replied,

"Well, there is something. Or rather there was, but it was a long time ago when I was in the Golden Dawn. To be frank, my memory fails me on a lot of things these days, especially things from so long ago. But as I recall I heard of one fellow who claimed to have made it [the Homunculus] and who was working to 'raise' it properly back then. This was back in London. He was a friend of one of our Order members, but refused to join the Order itself. He said he didn't trust the Chief or the Adepts of the Order, and so wanted to

have none of it. But as I said he was a friend of one of our group, and so the two discussed it closely, or so I was told. But that wasn't all.

"You know how rumors abound in this business, so when I heard about it from this other Order member, I didn't think too much about it at the time, except to find it fascinating. Frankly, though, I don't think I really believed any of it. But then I was shown a photograph of it, one taken by its maker. There was a yardstick directly behind the thing, and it was only about ten inches tall. But I have to tell you, it looked like a well-formed, perfect, miniature human. It didn't look like any fake or a doll or anything like that. No. It was so real, I felt that if I reached out and touched the photo, I'd feel living flesh. You could just see life in its eyes. Like I said, this was no fake. Everything about it was correct. It was so well proportioned. The head and fingers especially. Those tiny fingers looked just perfect, the right length, and so well-fitted to that peewee hand. Fascinating.

"Since that day I kept this memory to myself mostly, because it was so strange and I had got myself in enough trouble by releasing the GD material. But what I was really intrigued with was the fact that this fellow said there were magical techniques he was using to 'raise' and 'train' it. Of course, this really pulled me in. But I never heard about it or saw any more photos after that, as I left the Order a few months later. This is why I'm interested. Is such a thing possible, and if it is, does magic have any role in its upbringing? Really, about the closest I ever got to this subject was the Magical Child Rite we discussed so many years ago, and the paper I gave you on it. Now that you're on the verge of actually attempting this thing, well, you can see why I'm so interested."

I asked him if I could relate his tale to Frater, since the two of them were no longer communicating, and I would be contacting Frater to ask how to conduct the experiment. To this Regardie replied,

"Do what you want, but Albert already heard this story from me. We discussed it several times, and he told me about other cases he had heard of just like it. I have to tell you though, I sincerely believe that at the very least he has toyed with the idea of trying to create one himself. It was just the look on his face when we discussed it. I can't be sure, but I have a feeling he may actually have done at least some work on it. That German attitude of his and all, you know! But if he did, his Christian morality forced him to drop it. So now that he has you doing his work for him as usual, well, he won't worry. You'll carry his baggage for him!"

I didn't care for Regardie's attitude, and told him so. He retaliated, and the argument grew. Before we ended the conversation however, each of us backed off. There was too much at stake, and neither of us wanted to end our relationship this way. There had been too much of that with others throughout the history of Alchemy and Magic, and we did not want to become part of those casualty statistics. In the end, we just laughed off our sharp remarks.

Seeing that the *Generation* paper was now ready to submit, I contacted Frater about the Homunculus matter. I reminded him of our private conversation about it. I told him he said we would discuss the Homunculus matter when the time came, and that indeed, the time had come. He agreed, and asked me to telephone him that Sunday evening for

"...what will be a long and hard discussion. It is time you begin the work. Just make certain you have enough of the Gur left. The rest you can take care of easily enough. You have four days before our discussion. I want you to reflect deeply over the Gur, and on your own role in this process. Study Paracelsus carefully on the matter. You have completed the Water Work and generated the Homeric animals. Now, you must take on this new role. We will discuss all in detail Sunday night."

Over the next four days, I read and re-read the writings of Paracelsus regarding the Homunculus, and recalled that a spagyric substance was needed. Further, it continually occurred to me that this material most probably did refer to the male sperm, just as the encyclopedias had also stated. But the idea of spagyrics kept reoccurring to me to such an extent, that I finally wondered if its two root words, Spao (separate), and Ageiro (combine), had something else to do with the alchemical process that laid behind the work on the Homunculus. The more I considered it, the more certain I became there was something here. But just how did separation and combination apply to the process?

I kept considering Paracelsus' instruction to place these spagyric substances into a glass container, sealing it and burying it in horse dung for a period of forty days, and that at the end of that time, "...something would be found that would both be alive and which would move in the container," and further, as Paracelsus had stated, "...at times this would be a man; a Homunculus, but who had no body and indeed was transparent at that time." But all of this made no sense, at least, not at first.

Then I contemplated his remaining counsel on the matter:

"...regardless of these conditions, the creature yet exists, and it only remains for the Alchemist but to bring him up, a process that is no more difficult than that which was used to generate him. This 'raising process' may be accomplished by feeding the creature daily, over a period of 40 weeks, with the 'Arcanum' of human blood. But yet throughout this time, the forming creature must not be removed from the dung hill in which he was formed. At the end of this time there should be a living child, having every member as well-proportioned as any infant born of a human woman. He will be smaller and more frail than a normal human child though, and will require more care and attention in his education, with physical education being stressed."

Somewhere in all of this, it all came together. For now, I saw that the process of separation had been invoked during the putrefaction of the rain water, which had produced the Gur, and that the combination would occur when the male sperm—my sperm—would impregnate the Mother Gur. This must be the secret process, I thought, as all elements are accounted for, including not removing the vessel from the dung hill, which equates to the laboratory sand bath, kept at 98.6 degrees Fahrenheit, the temperature of the human body. That is, after fertilization, the vessel with the impregnated "Mother Earth" would have to be placed in a sand bath, and a human body temperature maintained in the sand bath throughout the 'gestation' period. It all fit.

There were leaps in logic in this thesis most certainly, but it all fit subjectively, and that is what is most important in these matters. Not reason, but internal perception. If these ideas were correct, then this occult process should result in a creature that appears as a miniature human being; one made from the 'Salt' of the Mother Earth, and which therefore would possess a physical body. Its Mercury, or Life, would come from its creator—its 'Father'—in this case, from myself. But such a being would not possess a Soul or consciousness in alchemical terms. It would be up to me to work with the creature, eventually imparting to it a purpose to fulfill. Such conjecture on my part during those early days also accounted for the fact that only a male alchemist was said to be able to create the Homunculus, as it is his seed that must impregnate the Mother Earth. Further, it became clear to me that after the impregnation, as with a human child, the cycle of development and growth would begin.

During that Sunday night telephone conversation, I began by proudly announcing to Frater Albertus the sum and substance of my thesis. To my absolute delight, he confirmed it completely. I informed him I had seventeen grams of Gur left after performing all of the Water Work, and that I prayed this quantity would be sufficient for starting this work. He explained to me that only four grams would be needed, and that I should save the rest for future trials. He cautioned:

> "It will not be easy. You will most likely suffer several false starts until you get the hang of it; particularly with properly supplying the growing fetus with the Arcanum of Blood and Air. For the rate at which the blood flow is regulated is crucial, as is the fact that the blood must come from you—and from no one else. You are the Father, and must 'extend' yourself in the mechanical procedures of nurturing by controlling the rate of blood flow to the fetus, just as the Gur will nurture by doing 'her' part, constantly, throughout the gestation period. Controlling the air flow will not be difficult as you will see. But controlling the blood flow, ah! There is the rub! Yet you can do it with great care and diligence."

We discussed the details of the experiment, including the design of the vessel that would serve as the 'womb' for the creature. It was not so much a difficult design as was the process behind its correct use. For as Frater explained to me,

> "The apparatus is not large. In fact, it stands no taller than six inches, has two side-arms for controlled air flow, and another side-arm for the injection of the Arcanum, which is only three inches in diameter. It must be placed in the dung hill—or as you correctly surmised, a sand bath—and buried halfway up the vessel and left there undisturbed for nine months. That is the only part of the process that is incorrect. I suspect Paracelsus and others who did this work purposely gave the wrong figure here to stop the idle curious from attempting this work. In fact, I suspect that is why Paracelsus states the creature has no body and will be transparent or invisible after 40 days, yet must still be worked with. This is a ruse. It takes every bit of nine months to create the creature—as you are about to find out.
>
> "Now as to the rate of fresh air flow. As I said, you have to be careful with it, but not so careful as with the rate of blood flow. I

recently saw a miniature electric air pump in a science catalog. Get the catalog and order it, and begin to work with it to get the feel of how it works and how to adjust it to give the proper air flow. It's so small it runs off batteries but it's ideal for this project. It provides just enough air movement to allow for refreshing the air in the 'womb' without disturbing the fetus. The rate of air flow should be no more than two feet per minute so the forming fetus is not disturbed, but is still aerated. You'll be able to tell the aeration is proceeding at the proper rate when small, lazy ripples appear and move across the surface of the Gur-sperm combination. Also, make certain that both rubber tube vents remain open during this Breathing Cycle. This allows the easy passage of air flow through the vessel, over the fetus, and out the exhaust port. This has to be done every seventy-two hours. No more, no less.

"There is something else. There is a great danger that the developing fetus will become contaminated with bacteria from the outside during the aeration process. Each of the rubber tube vents [or side-arms on the sides of the vessel] must be fitted with a ball airlock, the kind you used when fermenting your herbs for the Herbal Stone. You have to use it, because even though you aerate the fetus every three days, the vents must remain open to the air at all times during the nine-month gestation process. Gases will be evolved by the fetus during its development, and you will have to vent the vessel without letting any contaminants in. And be certain you use Potassium bisulfite in the ball-locks to kill any bacteria or mold that might enter through the open end of the locks. This is important. Sterility must be assured!"

My concerns were now with regulating the blood flow, so I impatiently interjected, "How is the flow of the Arcanum regulated? How often is it supplied to the fetus?" Frater replied,

"It is difficult. You will have to determine the exact rate for your case yourself. But as a general guideline only, you will use the third

side-arm of the vessel for adding the Arcanum. Add it with a hypodermic syringe, one hundred milliliters at a time. This will have to be done every three to seven days: you will have to determine that for yourself. How will you know it has received enough? Excess blood will begin to pool on top of the Gur. When that occurs, stop. When all of the pooled Arcanum has disappeared, and the surface of the Gur begins to take on a dry appearance, more must be added. But be careful. It is possible to add too much or add it too quickly, at which time the fetus will literally drown in the Arcanum—that is, in the very Life of which the blood is only the vehicle as you were taught in class."

I objected that such a small amount of Gur, four grams, could possible absorb so much blood. But Frater only laughed.

"When you get it right, you will see the foolishness of your academic objections. And you will pray that it doesn't take any more than you can give from yourself during any of the Feedings, as I call them!"

The additional questions I had were all answered by Frater during that two-hour discussion. At the end of the conversation he said,

"Begin as soon as you can, and good luck. Keep me informed every step of the way. If you have any problems you cannot solve yourself, or need some advice, get in contact with me as quickly as you can. This is much too important a work, so don't let anything get out of hand."

I was forthright about the matter, and explained to Frater that I would not only be informing Regardie of the details of our conversation, but would be keeping him apprised of any progress I might make, as closely as I would be him. Frater paused when I told him this and replied,

"Do what you will, but I think you are extending information to someone who will do nothing with it. You know where he and I stand, and you may very well consider using better judgment in this matter."

My thoughts immediately centered on Frater's abandonment of the furnace and its replication for his intended Paralab commercial sales of the Fixed and Unfixed Tinctures of Antimony, as well the abandonment of the temperature measurement determinations, the reproduction on the Water Work with the Van de Graaff I had sent him, not to mention some other matters that I was personally aware of that had fallen through on his end. But I said nothing. A breach already existed between Frater and Regardie, and I was now in the middle of it in a way, and wanted nothing further to do with what I saw as personality conflicts. My only response to his comment was to thank him and to tell him I would remember his words.

The next day I telephoned Regardie and told him the details of my conversation with Frater. He was both delighted and chagrined, as he muttered,

"So I was right after all. He does know what he's talking about, which means he attempted it as I thought he might have. And no doubt his morality caused him to drop it, because certainly he would not be looking to you to it carry through. You know how he is. If he can do it himself, then the hell with anyone else! He prefers to say it was by his efforts he got results, whatever the case may be. So obviously, he got so far with it and then dropped the whole matter. Let's face it. If he coined the terms, Breathing Cycle and Feedings in all this, then he did do the work. What a shame! What a damn shame he dropped the ball and left it go! But now it's your turn, so all I'll say is what he did. Good luck, and let me know how things go."

Throughout May and June, I ordered the special design of the vessel for the womb that Frater had given me, readied the equipment when it arrived, and began the experiments in August, 1982. From that time until early October, I failed three times, each time due to the problem of regulating the flow of the Arcanum into the grayish mass that formed when the Mother Gur was fertilized. Failure was easy to tell. The mass simply decayed in the vessel, giving off a horrible odor. The fourth time, in mid-October, 1982, success was achieved. An edited version of the procedure, taken from my notebook, **Experiments in Life and Death**, is as follows:

❈❈❈❈

Day 1
Beginning of Experiment

The Gur was sterilized using a standard Electron Bombardment technique. This time, not at 50,000 volts at 25 microamperes as was used in the Generation of Animals, but with 12,000 volts AC (Alternating Current) at 12 milliamperes. Bombardment time: 6 hours. The vessel (womb) was also sterilized using 12,000 volts AC. Exposure time: 6 hours. Using a proper Sterilization Chamber, the Gur was added to the vessel, and my own fresh semen (sperm) to impregnate the Gur, and the vessel sealed and placed in a sand bath at 98.6 degrees Fahrenheit.

Day 10

The Gur was fed twice already, and aerated twice as well, both times on Days 4 and 8. Frater was right. The grayish mass absorbs the Arcanum at such a rate I could hardly believe my eyes. There are no distinguishable features in the Gur yet. I suppose I expect to see something like an embryo. But with this work, I am not sure. Certainly, Frater was no help at all when I asked him this question. He would not give me a straight answer here except to laugh and tell

Israel Regardie & the Philosopher's Stone 195

me, "When you see what you see, you will tell me. Then you will join me in my knowledge, and this work will be carried on into the next generation," whatever the hell that means! All I see is a grayish mass lying on the bottom of the womb and nothing more. EXCEPT that the blood is absorbed by the mass, and the air that is removed through the evacuation side-arm of the vessel has a very distinct sweet odor, like the fragrance that arises from a field of flowers in the Spring. It certainly has not decayed as in the three previous experiments, and is, at least, something curious.

Day 30

Something is happening. Six days ago, I gave another feeding and aeration. The odor coming from the vessel during the evacuation phase of the aeration is so sweet as to be overpowering. It is, to my sense, sickeningly sweet. But that is not all. Using a bright light and a magnifying glass, I saw what appeared to be tiny red lines in the Gur. Markings if you will. The type one sees on a map, the details of which are taken by a satellite from space. It also appears that the grayish mass is turning a deeper gray in color, and that a black spot, the size of a very small pea, has appeared near the top part of the mass that is facing East in the sand bath. I have my opinions (or rather, ideas here) but don't want to prejudice my own mind with some fanciful misgivings. Time alone will tell.

Day 45

There is no question about it. The tiny red lines have become larger. To me, they look like capillaries. The (now) dark grayish mass has also taken on a shape. To me, it resembles a small, curled up fetus. I cannot see any hands or appendages of any kind, so simply note this. Additionally, the black pea-like structure has grown larger and more distinct. It has a very glossy appearance and is fixed into its position in the Gur. It appears to be an eye during its early formative stages, this as I remember such things from my undergraduate Zoology and Biology classes. The amount of Arcanum required has also increased. Until I see more progress, I will continue to call the grayish mass just that: a grayish mass. Having stated that, the grayish mass requires the administration of 170 milliliters of blood every 5 days, an increase. As always, the blood simply disappears into the mass. After 4 days, the outside edges of the mass begin to dry out, but only lightly. By the fifth day, there is a gentle dry appearance on the surface of the mass. At this time, I add further Arcanum. Thus, I have the processes of aeration or Breathing as Frater has termed the process, down, as well as the proper time between Feedings. At least, for now. For certainly, as this mass grows…if it does grow any further…I expect the times between aerations and feedings to decrease. My only concern is will I be able to supply enough of the Arcanum to keep the experiment going.

Day 60

There can be no doubt about it. The red markings are capillaries, their transparency being given away by concentrations of blood in them, at different points, as the Arcanum courses through them. Additionally, the pea-like object has lost its glossy color. It is now flat-black in appearance, and has grown larger. I estimate it is now the size of a large pea, or even a small bean. But there is something else as well. The dark grayish mass has definitely increased in size over the past 10 days. I estimate it has increased its size by 30%. The amount of blood required during feeding, however, has remained the same: 170 ml. The times between aeration has also remained the same: feeding every 5 days, aeration, every 4 days.

Day 90

There is so much condensation inside the vessel I can't be sure about what I think I'm seeing. No doubt, the water content of the semen and sperm has given rise to this fog. Up until 5 days ago, this condensation has always remained on the bottom one-third of the vessel. Not anymore. The entire womb is so fogged-up, I can't tell what is happening with any certainty. Aeration and feeding have been going on as normal. I trust the feeding time, since the Gur still dries out over its surface, or seems to as best as I could visually determine, just as before, although I can't see the surface of the Gur mass very clearly due to the condensation. Frater told me to just continue with things as usual. He said the condensate should clear up shortly, and then I "...would see something wonderful..." We shall see.

Day 120

The condensation cleared up 15 days ago, and it is now obvious that the mass has taken on the shape of a crescent, although the points of the crescent at the top and bottom are rounded, somewhat like a more distinct fetus. There seems to be some pulsing in it, but I can't be sure. It's just too dark down in the vessel, and the added light I use only causes greater glare when trying to make out such delicate vertical movements. But there is something else also. I couldn't believe my eyes, but Frater told me it was the "something wonderful" he told me about last month. There are two tiny appendage-like projections near the center of the mass, and at the ends of them, what looks to be even tinier small humps or bumps. These are the "...arms and hands, those humps or bumps as you call them, are miniature fingers..." he explained. Aeration periods remain the same, but the feeding time has increased, while the amount of the Arcanum used to feed it has decreased. Now only 130 ml of the Arcanum is administered every 7 days. It's a good thing too. It's getting difficult supplying the Life so often. My diet has changed to include mostly red meats, and I have started taking megavitamins to keep up with the demand. Still, I feel fine. I think my concern is really more of a psychological matter than it is a physical one.

Day 150

Great progress has been made. There is no cloudiness or condensate in the vessel whatsoever, and the dark grayish mass has turned a light gray, making it fairly easy to see what is going on down in the vessel when a strong light is used. Clearly, the appendages are miniature arms, and the ends possess finger-like growths. The eye has a film over it, much like an actual eyelid, and there *is* a pulsating, up and down motion to it. I have tried to take photographs of the creature using my German Practika 35 mm camera outfit, but I cannot get the resolution I need. Even the PL+3 close-up lenses cannot resolve what is going on down in the bottom of the vessel. At least I have the hand drawings I made. That will have to be enough.

Aeration has continued according to schedule, and the administration of the Arcanum has also dropped again over the last 30 days. Now, only 90 ml of blood is required, and that, still, only every 7 days. It is strange though. The mass has increased approximately 50% over and above the earlier 30% increase, yet less blood is required. Frater told me, "...you have to remember there has not been enough work done in this area, so we don't know if this is normal or not. But continue on as best you can..." This seems to be an about face for him. My interpretation is that he took this experiment only so far as Regardie speculated, and had to abort it. That's why he can no longer guide me on what is happening in my experiment. As far as I am concerned, I am on my own now, and will just have to feel my way as I go. Nevertheless, in my opinion, things are looking up!

Day 180

Something is wrong. Everything has changed over the past 6 days. The mass I refer to as a creature at the bottom of the vessel had turned a very dark gray, a brownish color appearing around the rim of the crescent. There is only a slight pulsation as well, and the eye, as I can make it out through its lid, seems smaller. I continued the aeration as usual, and on day 5 (of the 6 since I noticed something amiss) I increased the supply of the Arcanum back up to 130 ml. I will continue this every 5 days, using both fresh and stored blood I saved from earlier blood draws. It just feels right at this point, because the thing may truly be starving. I don't know what else to do, hence my decision to increase the food supply. All of it has been absorbed by the thing however, but the color change disturbs me. I think it is dying. Perhaps the increased quantity of Arcanum and the decreased time between feedings will bring it back to health.

Day 220

The Experiment has ended. The thing died two days ago. I have not been able to face this failure, especially when I consider how much I gave to it in terms of everything that was required. Even though I continued to aerate as usual and feed it every 5 days, it was not enough. Two days ago, when I started to aerate, the odor of death emerged from the exhaust sidearm of the vessel. The stench of death is unmistakable, and heaven knows, I have smelled it so many times in my life, that there was no doubt of it. When examined with a bright light, the crescent-shaped mass was very dark brown, almost black, motionless, and lacked any and all definition. The arms, fingers, and eye had disappeared, being returned to the Gur. I tried adding more Arcanum immediately, and sat with the experiment for 38 hours continuously, trying to monitor the rate of blood flow so as not to kill it by feeding it too fast, if indeed, it was not already dead. Aeration was also increased, as a last effort to revive what I had created. But it all failed. When I removed the vessel from the sand bath and opened it, the stench of death was so powerful, that I jumped back. It was the most powerful death smell I ever experienced. I could not bring myself to clean the vessel by discarding the thing as though it was a piece of garbage. As strange as it is to write this, I felt and still do feel a great emotional attachment to the little thing, and cried when I realized it died. I feel I loved it in some way. I buried the vessel with the creature in the woods, and retreated to my laboratory until today. I feel so badly the poor thing had to die, and die the way it did. It never had a chance at life in the world, and I am beyond grief in knowing this. I don't think I will ever forgive myself for not being able to give it a life it deserved.

When I called Frater a few hours ago and told him what happened, he too felt very sad, and expressed such to me. In his words, "...many would fault us for what we have done. But all of this is God's Plan for mankind, and in the whole, this work has its place too. We could have learned so much, and become so much closer to the Creator if we could have succeeded in this Grand Experiment..." I felt the same too. Both of us were choked up. We had to end the telephone call abruptly.

I will have to contact Regardie as soon as I am able, and explain what happened to my creation. I have no idea how he will take it. And frankly, I don't give a damn.

❊❊❊❊

The following week I discussed the matter with Regardie. Till this day, I am not certain who took my failure harder: Regardie or Frater Albertus. He told me that he had hopes because of this work, and that he actually believed the Experiment could be pulled off successfully. He looked for the creature being brought to term as he put it, so it could finally be brought into the world. Because if so, if this could be accomplished, all would somehow be well. As he continued to speak, I could hear he was adamant in his conviction that Magic would play at least some role in its maturation and development, since it was a creation brought forth by occult means to begin with. Somehow, through all of his disappointment, I felt he needed something fresh to hold on to; something that would justify his lifelong dedication to Magic. A dedication to a pursuit that had not fulfilled its promises to him in any complete way, in the same way that it had failed to fulfill all of its promises to the rest of us who spent so much of our lives justifying our activities in it. And of course, that Magic was the Magic of the New Age, with all of its many offshoots, most of which could be traced back directly to the Golden Dawn System.

Both Regardie and I, as well as Frater and I, never spoke of the matter again. To this day, I feel it was more painful for each of us than we knew or could accept at the time, since each of us—and for our own reasons—wanted so much for this work to succeed.

It was the middle of May, 1983. Everything had changed. The 'Grand Experiment' had ended in failure. Somewhere in all of those seven months of intense work in trying to bring the Homunculus into the world, I determined that my place was no longer at the steel company at which I had been employed for almost ten years as an Electrical Engineer. I had a great longing inside, one that had to be fulfilled at all costs. And that longing was to return to university and seek additional degrees.

I resigned from my position, my wife and I broke up our home, and we moved to other places in order for me to continue with my education. In keeping with these new plans, my entire alchemical laboratory, along with all of the accomplishments in which I had succeeded—*e.g.,* the four Herbal Stones, the various Unfixed and Fixed Tinctures of Antimony, the Green Lion, the Red and Yellow Kermes, the Kirkrum Menstruum, the various colored glasses of Antimony, and an assorted sundry of other products—were packed up and placed into storage, where they remain to this day. I felt then—and still do—that all that is important is my knowledge and experience in this field. And if the occasion should arise, I can resurrect the laboratory at will—and do what needs to be done.

After earning my degrees, I buried myself in my own scientific research in which I am engaged to this day. Combined with my private occult work, writing, and students, there has simply not been any time to pursue any further alchemical laboratory work. Thus ended the years of constant, continuous activity in my pursuit of Alchemy. As to Regardie's and Frater Albertus' involvement? The next and final chapter of this book will address this issue.

Chapter Nine

Clouds on the Alchemical Horizon

In the fall of 1983, my wife and I had moved on, the failure of the Grand Experiment still being too painful a matter for me to think about. At the same time, as had been the case throughout the previous twelve years, Regardie and I kept in close contact. In one of the discussions in the Fall of that year, Regardie told me,

"To be frank with you, Joe, I'm pretty well sick of the whole thing. I've spent the last fifty-six years of my life studying, learning, practicing, and defending Magic and the Golden Dawn, and so many years in the pursuit of Alchemy, that I don't even know exactly when the spark of that idea first entered my mind.

"And for what? Yes, I suppose I can credit Magic with this and Alchemy with that, because of what I know and experienced in all of it. But really, when push comes to shove, I can't cite a single instance where I can attribute this result to that cause, or that effect to some other cause. It's the way it is. One just never knows in this business! Now I just want to enjoy the remaining years of my life. So much lost! So many mistakes, so many misgivings. No, I'm not saying I missed being a playboy, because I would never have wanted to waste my life like that. But I can tell you one thing for certain. I would have damn well liked to have experienced what it was like to be one! If only for a while! But that's not the way things turned out."

To me he sounded as if he regretted the way he went in life, recalling some of his misgivings he mentioned to me throughout the years. This time however, it was different somehow. There was genuine depression or masked severity in his voice; the type a man gets when—sitting in his easy chair in the wee hours of the morning—shadows of his life and thoughts relentlessly creep across the screen of his mind during his reflections. So, I asked him if he had it to do all over again, what would he have done? His reply was telling to say the least.

"Well, first off, I would never have gotten involved with that Blavatsky material when I was still a teenager, around seventeen years old. And I can tell you, I would have gotten a better education, one in physics, or chemistry, or even astronomy. And all this Magic business? I don't know. I think I would have liked to—maybe—puss around with it a bit, if I did discover it again a second time around, but never again would I take it as far as I did. It just leaves you empty and shriveled up inside when all is said and done.

"Look at Crowley! I spent the greater part of my life defending him! In a way, I don't really regret it. But at the same time, the older I get, the harder the facts become! Or should I say, the clearer they become, because now I'm looking in my own mirror! Look how he ended up! And his followers today? They try to rewrite his ending as if it was some type of glorious completion to a noble life! What the hell is wrong with them! Trying to make silk purses out of a sow's ear, that's what people in this Magic business try to do! If chaps like you want to continue with it, that's your business. But as for me, I learned what I learned, and here is where I'm at as a result of all of it.

"Oh, sure, I'll keep my fingers in it now that I've come this far, watching what Temples rise here and there, giving a bit of advice and help when asked. I try to do this for the few groups trying to get going in this country, in England, and down under. And I'm going to continue to write and pass along what I think should be passed

along to the next generations. But as far as getting actively involved in any of it personally, to the breadth and depth I did in the old days? Never! That's for the young ones, if they want to invest the best years of their lives in these things. You see, Joe, at the end of the day, all of this has become bittersweet to me. Hell, a fellow can't even make up his mind how he feels about things when it comes right down to it; and that includes his own life and what he did with it! Magic ties you up into so many knots, you can't find the beginning or end of the string! It's always that way. A mixture. That's why I say it's bittersweet!

"There are some other personal things I don't like to talk about that I would take care of the next time around, and properly, too. Things that have always bothered me, but which my family was negligent in seeing were done for me when I was very young. It's too personal to get into, even with you, but I was not treated fairly by them in certain things that were fundamental as far as my world view and my feelings about who I am goes.

"As to Alchemy and Albert? Lord, I wish I never heard of them! But again, in the early days, things between he and I were so good. Oh! How good they were! There were many days and nights we worked together so well at the Rose-Croix. How I remember those days, and the fondness I have for them and for Albert is second to none. But as you know, as the years wore on so did we, and in the end, well, you know how that one ends, too.

"I would also have liked to have a stable and lasting marriage, and a child or two. Probably two. I missed that. Oh, sometimes I say I'm glad I never had any of the little urchins; but you know, between you and me, there are times I deeply regret not having experienced fatherhood. Sometimes I think that denying fatherhood has left an unfilled need for completeness. It's probably mainly a biological need, but no one had better try to tell me that's all it is, because I'll smash them in the mouth, even if I am an old man! Really, I think procreation is all part of the human package of experience, and *those who don't fulfill the role will suffer for it in their later years. You and your wife will see what I mean, if you don't have a child or two. Mark me!*

"The other thing I would have liked to have had was a good, solid career in something the world paid top dollar for, without having to carve out a living from something no one understands, society is disagreeable to—well, at least it's becoming better now than it was back in the old days—and most folks just don't give a damn about. Don't get me wrong. I made a good living at what I did and I helped many people. I know this. Well, at least I think I helped them and that's what really matters. But what really bothers me about this psychotherapy business is the same thing that bothers me about Magic. You can never really know whether your actions cause a given effect, if the whole damn thing is a science as some claim, or if it's something no one really understands. Because the truth is, no one really knows. Why do you think they have so many different schools of thought, each one having different interpretations of any given psychological abnormality or condition?

"In your field, light is light and gravity is gravity, and you have one or two theories that support and actually complement each other and which explain them, and how they work! You can even predict what's going to happen by using the equations! Try that with this psychology business! Can't use equations in my field! No, sir! You can never know. All this bothers me."

I was very grateful to Regardie for his candor, and that he willingly shared his thoughts with me. For in the end, actually, from late 1983 onward, a Teacher-student relationship no longer existed between us. Rather, the relationship flowered into a deep and lasting friendship. We continued our close contact every week, yes. But after 1983, until his demise in March of 1985, our conversations were about nothing but general life problems and concerns, and the subjects of Magic or Alchemy only broke up the flow of these everyday topics that had become the sum and substance of our talks.

Israel Regardie & the Philosopher's Stone

The relationship between Frater Albertus and I had changed in the opposite way however. After the failure of the Homunculus, I had difficulty reaching Frater from the Fall of 1983 onward. At first I thought it was because of my failure in the Grand Experiment. But the Secretary of the College—who served in that capacity throughout my entire Seven Year Cycle of Classes—told me otherwise. Olive v.d.M. and I had become fast friends throughout the years. Owing to this, in a series of telephone conversations from July 1983 through January 1984, she explained to me what happened.

Olive told me that Frater's attempt to downscale the classes into a three-year program had failed. In fact, she stated that he originally wanted to make them a four-year program, but for reasons that were unclear to her, he was unable to do this. However, even the three-year program failed, according to Olive. As she explained, the student applications for admission were simply not there. People were no longer applying to the College. As few as three or four would apply for a given class—sometimes only two—which was not enough in Frater's opinion to justify the amount of energy and work he would have to put into those classes. She said he felt that he needed to initiate enough people who would not only continue on with the work, but who would be available to expand the College and bring the rest of it as he had planned, into existence. She said,

"Even as early as the late Fall of 1982, you could tell something was wrong. People weren't interested anymore. At least, that's how it looked to me. Even the older ones from around the area here didn't drop by the way they used to. I felt that it was all coming to an end.

"I told Frater I thought that the day of Alchemy was over. That the world was entering a more materialistic phase, as he had predicted in his Men and the Cycles of the Universe book, and that because of this people like us were becoming redundant. He became upset with me, wouldn't hear of it, and continued to try and struggle onward. He tried so hard to combine people from, say, the first-year

class of February with the first-year class of September in order to come up with the numbers he needed to increase the size of the class and to further his own plans. But more often than not this failed due to people's schedules. All I'm doing now is paperwork that's meant to be important sometime in the future, as Frater says. Beside this, there is so little revenue coming in now from Paralab that Frater had to let some people go, and even mentioned to me he was going to have to put me on part-time soon. The atmosphere here is very heavy, and everyone but Frater is very depressed!"

When I told Regardie about these developments, he replied,

"Well, if I were interested anymore I would be upset. But this had to be, because it's the way Albert is. He never learned to complete one task and stabilize it thoroughly before attempting another. But I agree with Olive. In fact, I have been thinking the same thing since I got that letter from him which I just threw away without opening. It's all over. The day of Alchemy has passed. For how long? Who knows! But she is right. The world is moving on into dire materialism. I consider it no less than the dialectical materialism that forms the basis of Marxism, it's that severe. Maybe you too have finally learned your lesson. Remember me pulling your bacon out of Albert's fire last year? You see, it's over. Time for you to do what I have done—move on!"

The incident to which Regardie referred was an event that brought Frater and me to an impasse. For although the letter which catalyzed this event was dated May 19, 1982, I could not even broach what it offered me at that point. After all, it was received at the time I was to begin the experimental work on the Homunculus. In that letter, Frater offered me the position of "Director of Research of Phameres." Without even thinking about all of the demands I already had on my available time and schedules, I signed the Letter of Offer from Frater on June 22, 1982, and was about to return it to him when, for some reason, I discussed the matter with Regardie first. I was so mentally congested at the time, that I had blocked the issue out of my mind completely, and only when Frater had called and urged me to sign it and return it to him immediately, did I suddenly realize the predicament I was in. So, what to do? Of course. Ask Regardie.

It would be safe to say that Regardie lost it. Aside from the expletives, he asked me if I had forgotten about my desire to return to university next year; if I forgot that he had helped me make some financial investments that would assure my wife and I had an easier time during the first few years of my schooling; if I had forgotten about the furnace fiasco, the donation of so much equipment to the PRS (of which the Van de Graaff was only one of the many pieces of equipment named in this book); the problems he had with Frater throughout decades; the Water Work I had just gone through for several years and what that required of me; and now the "...mess you have in preparing for this Homunculus experiment and God only knows how this will end and what it will take from you..."

Then he reminded me that this would necessitate not only abandoning my plans, but moving across the country to Salt Lake City. He went on with,

"...he'll stick you in that small house on the property, you'll be working your tail off from sunup to sunset at Paralab and Phameres, and on the Homunculus work that he'll still want you to do on your own, in one of his labs. There won't be any time for anything let alone furthering your education, and your wife will wind up helping him in some other way. In the meantime, either you or she or both of you will have to augment the pittance of a salary he might—and Joe, listen to me when I say, might—pay you just to make ends meet! Is this want you want? Because if it is, take it, but don't bother calling me again!"

This time Regardie got through to me. Because of his words, I finally saw the light, saw what I was about to lose for another of

Frater's dreams, and it pulled me up dead in my tracks. I told Francis I would take care of the matter by declining the Phameres position, and carry out the Homunculus work on my own. With that, he applauded and said,

"I'm sorry if I was rough on you, but you deserved it and I meant every word. Sometimes there's no other way to reach you than to get tough. You're an Obsessive-Compulsive, or so I see it, and that's what it takes. It usually doesn't do much good when you get tough with your type, but at least with you, it works every once in a while. And thank God, it worked now!"

The following day I telephoned Frater and told him I had decided to decline the offer. Regardie had speculated correctly. Frater tried to talk me into reconsidering. He told me about the important research this new arm of the College would undertake, and the role I would be able to play in it; he suggested I go to night school at the University of Utah at Salt Lake, and after completing my masters, I would "... *probably* have enough free time from your Phameres duties to enable you to pursue a Doctorate full time. I'll help you all I can after the start-up phase is over, so you should have no problems." I asked if that was a guarantee. He replied, honestly,

"Well, no. You know how these things go. It's going to take a lot of work for several years. And those of us on the ground floor will have to work day and night to make it a reality. But of course, we don't know how long that will take. But it can be done, if people like you are willing to commit themselves to it."

It was then that I patently refused. I stated I would continue on with the Homunculus Experiment, but was going back to university at all costs, and that was that. He accepted my decision grudgingly, but at least he accepted it. From that point on, we never spoke of the matter again, even during the times I consulted him during the work on the Homunculus. When I told Regardie about all of this, he was as delighted as he was angry with me that day I called asking for his advice in the matter.

In February of 1984 I received a telephone call from Olive. In a low, matter-of-fact voice she said,

"Joe, earlier today Frater gave me a list of seven people he wanted me to call. You're on the list, so I'm calling to tell you that Frater has colon cancer. It's inoperable. He only has a few weeks to live."

I cannot recall my thoughts during those moments, as the gravity of her words pulled me down into some type of mental oblivion. All I recall is being lost in thought that day. The following day Regardie telephoned me. "I suppose Olive called you, too?" he asked. I told him yes. We barely said a dozen words between us during the few minutes the call lasted. All I recall Regardie saying is, "It shouldn't have ended this way."

In July, 1984 I received another telephone call from Olive. I was attending a physics conference in Philadelphia. All she said was,

"Joe, I'm calling to tell you that Frater passed away a little more than an hour ago. Soror Emmy asked me to let a small group of you know. A public announcement will be made this week."

While I expected to hear this, nothing can prepare one for the actual event. I left the conference, returned to our small apartment near the University of Maryland, and left the matter alone for the next two years. Finally, in 1986, I returned to Salt Lake City on a private matter. After taking care of my business there, I visited Soror Emmy. She was delighted to see me. And for a brief while, we were able to capture some of the excitement and joy that was the former Paracelsus Research Society, the alchemical work done there, and to remember the powerful personality that was Frater Albertus. It was during that conversation that she told me,

"Albert was diagnosed with the condition in early 1983, but he refused to be treated for it. He said his work was done now, and that it was time he went on to other work and other places."

That was the last time I spoke with Soror. She too passed on a few years after that.

In January 1985, I was very short on funds. The educational expenses were growing, and there was very little extra money to spare for anything else. Due to this, Regardie and I had only two telephone conversations between January to March of 1985. During the January discussion we chatted mainly about daily life affairs, my progress at university, and how he was enjoying his new life in Sedona, Arizona. Finally, I asked him about Frater's passing. His only words were,

"What he did, he did. What he gave to all of us who would listen, he gave. I wish it had gone differently between he and I. But Albert was a stubborn German, and I'm an equally stubborn Jew. I suppose it couldn't have ended any other way, really, when you think back over all of it."

For some reason, even though my wife and I were so flat broke, on March 10, 1985, I found myself with a pocketful of change. I walked to a pay telephone—we could not even afford to have a telephone in our tiny apartment in those days—and telephoned Regardie.

Regardie told me he missed being able to call because we did not have a telephone, and that his life was going along. But he was "...not very happy these days. Youth is wasted on the young! I don't have the energy anymore, and it's actually hard to try to have a good time! Can you imagine that?" He went on, "...you know, I feel shitty these last few weeks. But I'm going out to dinner tonight with some friends. Maybe that will make me feel better." That was the last time I spoke with Francis. For on that night, as I would find out from C. S. Hyatt a month later, Regardie died of a massive heart attack at dinner that very night. To this day, I am glad the gods gave me that one last conversation with him, the very day he died.

Thus ended the life and times of Dr. Francis Israel Regardie. Neither the world of Magic nor the world at large will ever be the same without him, nor will it ever forget him.

And Thus It Is Finished

Epilogue

This, then, was the man, Magician, and Alchemist, Francis Israel Regardie. The world will never see another like him. Through his love of Magic and Alchemy, and his overwhelming devotion to them, he gave so much, that those yet unborn will find value and merit in what he stood for, not only through his writings, but through the very force of his life. A life that refused to accept the going standard, and one that pushed into the furthest recesses of the unknown by traveling to the outer limits of human experience.

I have done my best to give as honest, accurate, and clear presentation as I could of Regardie and his life, along with the work he had achieved in Alchemy. At the same time, I have struggled to give as complete a description of his intense interactions with Frater Albertus and myself in this occult field of investigation.

To be sure, there will be those who will argue this point and that, who disagree with this statement or that conclusion. Let them. For this was Regardie as I knew him throughout the last fourteen years of his life. This was the Regardie who not only knew and worked with the man, Frater Albertus, during the earliest days of the latter's beginning through to his end, but who taught Regardie his Alchemy, as he taught me mine. To my mind, these are more than sufficient credentials for me to speak through this book, and to lay down that which has not been know about Regardie—and about Frater Albertus for that matter—until now.

I am also certain there will be those who will wish this book was never written. To them I say, not one word, not one sentence, idea, or thought will be changed in this book to serve the monstrosities of political correctness, social responsibility, public image, or fear of this or that. It will remain exactly as it is. And what would Regardie say to those who idealize men of renown in order to make those men a part of their own narrow-minded transcendental occult world view? Someone whose name they can drop at their next lodge meeting or secret occult tea party as if they knew him and were walking in his footsteps? Ah, well! That's an easy one! I know what he would say. The same thing he stated to me on so many occasions, when the demon-headed hydra of self-illusion, self-delusion, and convenience reared its ugly head: "Joe, let them all go to Hell!"

NON-FICTION TITLES FROM JOSEPH LISIEWSKI

CEREMONIAL MAGIC & THE POWER OF EVOCATION

For centuries the ceremonial evocation of spiritual beings has been the single topic of the most famous "Grimoires"—and Magic's darkest corner. But the simplest of these, the *Heptameron* of Peter de Abano, has escaped the attention of modern Ceremonialists. Nonetheless, Its simplicity and power is second to none and *Ceremonial Magic & the Power of Evocation* lays its operation bare.

KABBALISTIC HANDBOOK FOR THE PRACTICING MAGICIAN
A Course in the Theory and Practice of Western Magic

For the practicing Magician there is no more crucial working knowledge than the Kabbalah. Yet none of the books on Kabbalah give the on-the-spot attributions, correspondences and key concepts in a user-friendly fashion. Until now. *Kabbalistic Handbook* gives you the tools to work Magic flawlessly...every time!

NON-FICTION TITLES FROM JOSEPH LISIEWSKI

HOWLINGS FROM THE PIT
A Practical Handbook of Medieval Magic, Goetia & Theurgy

Howlings lays bare what practical magic is all about. A veritable modern magical 'grammar,' *Howlings* takes you step-by-step through the mental, psychological & physical preparations required by the 'Fathers of the Grimoires', the authors of the classical books on ceremonial magic. Dr. Lisiewski clarifies dozens of technical points critical to successful magical operations—including evoking a spirit to physical manifestation!

KABBALISTIC CYCLES & THE MASTERY OF LIFE

Kabbalistic Cycles explains hidden universal laws known to but a few. With the knowledge of these strange cycles—and the detailed, step-by-step explanation of their use—you will know when to act in all matters, instantly. You will be able to discover the hidden agendas of others, and see every opportunity and adversity for what it really is. More than anything, you will attain what has been the goal of mankind: Mastery Over Your Own Life.

THE *Original* FALCON PRESS

Invites You to Visit Our Website:
originalfalcon.com

At our website you can:

- Browse the online catalog of all of our great titles
- Find out what's available and what's out of stock
- Get special discounts
- Order our titles through our secure online server
- Find products not available anywhere else including:
  – One of a kind and limited availability products
  – Special packages
  – Special pricing
- Get free gifts
- Join our email list for advance notice of New Releases and Special Offers
- Find out about book signings and author events
- Send email to our authors
- Read excerpts of many of our titles
- Find links to our authors' websites
- Discover links to other weird and wonderful sites
- And much, much more

Visit us today at originalfalcon.com

www.ingramcontent.com/pod-product-compliance
Lightning Source LLC
LaVergne TN
LVHW011935070526
838202LV00054B/4656